SPIRITUAL
BREAKTHROUGH

SPIRITUAL BREAKTHROUGH

Handbook

to

God-Consciousness

John Van Auken

ARE
PRESS

ASSOCIATION FOR
RESEARCH AND
ENLIGHTENMENT

A.R.E. Press • Virginia Beach • Virginia

First Published by Inner Vision Publishing
Second Printing by A.R.E. Press, October 1998
Printed in the U.S.A.

A.R.E. Press
215 67th Street
Virginia Beach, VA 23451-2061

Library of Congress Cataloging-in-Publication Data
Van Auken, John.
Spiritual breakthrough : handbook to God-consciousness
/ by John Van Auken.
    p.   cm.
Originally published: Virginia Beach, Va. : Inner Vision Pub.,
© 1992.
ISBN 0-87604-367-8
1. Spiritual life. 2. Cayce, Edgar, 1877-1945. 3. Association
for Research and Enlightenment. I. Title.
BP605.A77V36 1996
291.4—dc20   96-9706

Contents

Illustrations

INTRODUCTION

I was born to parents of two distinct approaches to God. My father found God in Nature and encouraged me to "feel" God throughout Nature. I can remember childhood moments—while camping in the woods and even while waiting quietly on a golf course—of feeling an underlying oneness in everything around me. I also remember catching glimpses of my father in quiet moments with that look in his eye as he was feeling Nature's presence. On the other hand, my mother was an urban, Irish-Catholic girl who found God through the ritual and wonder of her church's services, the old-style Catholic services, with dim candle-lit sanctuaries, the air filled with incense, praying and chanting in low tones, bells and reenactments of the passion of the Messiah. She took me to special ceremonies and novenas at night in small chapels that were simply magical to my young mind—flickering candlelight, exotic smells, bowed heads, Spirit-evoking prayers and rituals. I can remember moments when I thought everyone in the chapel was of one mind, one purpose, one attunement, and that at any moment God was going to appear and our hearts would burst from the wonder of it all.

But in all my spiritual learning I never found the depth and quality of instruction that I found in the Edgar Cayce legacy (see Appendix for background on him). When it came to answering questions about God and man, and how to consciously become aware of God, nothing had the depth, breadth and detail that the Cayce material did. Even when Cayce instructed studying the Bible to understand fully the spiritual path, he explained and supplemented it in such a way that it came alive for me. And it was Cayce who instructed seekers to go beyond the written material in books, to go directly to the Source, the mind of God, and consciously learn from God, as the prophets and saints had done. The idea of directly contacting God's consciousness, and being taught directly by God was an idea that lit up my mind. All of my adult life I have been, in varying degrees of intensity, seeking that direct consciousness of God's presence, God's voice, God's communication to me.

This book is an effort to share some of what I found along the way. Looking back over these many years of seeking God-consciousness, I can say that it has been an amazing, oftentimes surprising journey. The experiences were worth the effort and changes required for a finite, individualistic person to commune with the infinite, universal God. It is a path of paradoxical truths, a path of perpendicular dimensions. Experiencing humanity and divinity simultaneously requires an adroit

balancing of realities in order to hold to sanity throughout the process. But in the end, it is natural and comfortable, making life more meaningful, more enjoyable. The
result is a deep, quiet happiness, an enduring peaceful-
ness. Mortality is having no Infinite, Eternal connection.
Once that connection is made, there is no death, no limitation. The magic pill for all that ails us is a conscious
connection with Life Itself. Then It flows through us, fills
us, nourishes us. The contentment that results from this
is beyond imagining.

1

GOD-CONSCIOUSNESS

*S*piritual breakthrough is about God-consciousness. The goal is to reach a level of consciousness that allows us to be as aware of God as of ourselves. Imagine being as aware of God as we are of ourselves. This is the breakthrough we seek. But it is a difficult goal to realize. One of the greatest seekers of God-consciousness, the late Edgar Cayce teaches: "Remember there is no shortcut to a consciousness of the God-force. It is part of your own consciousness, but it cannot be realized by the simple desire to do so. Too often there is the tendency to want it and expect it without applying spiritual truth through the medium of mental processes. This is the only way to reach the gate. There are no shortcuts in metaphysics.

Life is learned within self. You don't profess it, you learn
it."[1]

Seekers of God-consciousness may include many
more people than we imagine. Edgar Cayce considered
people from many different backgrounds as true seekers of God-consciousness. He actually identifies certain
biblical names and terms as codes for something much
broader than we normally consider. As in the following
quote: "This is the meaning, this should be the understanding to all: Those that *seek* are Israel. 'Think not to
call thyselves the promise in Abraham. Know ye not that
the Lord is able to raise up children of Abraham from the
very stones?' So Abraham means *call;* so Israel means
those who seek. How obtained the supplanter [Jacob] the
name Israel? He wrestled with the angel, and he was face
to face with seeking to know His way. So it is with us that
are called and seek His face—We are Israel!"[2]

In order to understand the nature of this breakthrough, we need to be familiar with our god-seeking
heritage. Jews, Christians and Moslems all trace their
heritage to Abraham and include the biblical stories in
their religious literature. Let's review some great Bible
stories and teachings, using Edgar Cayce's insights to
help us gain a deeper understanding of the grand vista
of God, man and woman, and God-consciousness.

Two Keys to Understanding Biblical Stories

In order to understand the mystical messages in the
Bible, we need to keep two principles in mind as we read
it.

First, the Bible is not only a historical record of a specific group of people, but is also *an allegory for each individual soul's journey.* It is a vision into the passages
that *each* soul goes through in its quest for full enlight-

enment and eternal life. Therefore, when we read we should try to receive the stories as though they were personal insights and messages for ourselves, recalling our own past and foreshadowing our future. How can this be our past when we have only lived a short while? Because our *souls* have been alive from the beginning. As Jesus said, "Before Abraham was, I am."[3] So too were we alive. In the Cayce discourses we find many supporting examples of this truth. Here are a few examples:

> *The entity was in the beginning*, when the Sons of God came together to announce to Matter a way being opened for the souls of men, the souls of God's creation . . . [4]

> In the beginning . . . when the morning stars sang together, and the whispering winds brought the news of the coming of man's indwelling . . . and man became the living soul—*the entity came into being with this multitude.*[5]

> For in the beginning, God said, 'Let there be light.' *You are one of those sparks of light*, with all the ability of Creation, with all the knowledge of God.[6]

The Bible stories are *our* stories. We should read them as personal stories.

Second, the Bible contains not only the records of *physical* activities, it also contains metaphors of *inner-life* passages that occur as one awakens to the Kingdom of God (is) within (you).[7] When a seemingly outer physical activity is described in a Bible story, let's consider what it might mean to our inner process of spiritual breakthrough—as though it were a dream, carrying a message behind the outer story. The physical becomes symbolic of something deeper and, as a dream or parabole, it requires intuitive interpretation.

With these concepts in mind—namely, that the stories and teachings are *personal* and about *inner-life* processes—let's review some of the key stories in the Old and New Testaments. This background is important to our fuller understanding of the spiritual breakthrough process.

The Nature of God

THE COLLECTIVE

Genesis begins, "In the beginning God ("Elohiym" pronounced 'Aloheme') created the heavens and the earth. The Hebrew word "Elohiym" is a plural noun for "Deity." The use of the plural form reflects the collective, wholistic nature of God. When Elohiym speak, "they" refer to themselves in the plural, such as: "Let *us* make him in *our* image, according to *our* likeness."[8] Thus, Elohiym is not a singular, supreme entity separate from the creation. God is the Collective, composed of the created ones while at the same time their source. We actually contribute to the composition of God. That is not to say that we compose all of God's being, but simply to say that a portion of God's being is us.

This truth is expressed in many of the Cayce readings. In one example, Cayce encourages one seeker to come to know that not only God is God but self is a portion of that Oneness.[9]

As Jesus explained to Philip, "He who has seen me has seen the Father; how can you say, 'Show us the Father'? Do you not believe that I am in the Father and the Father in me? The words that I say to you I do not speak on my own authority; but the Father who dwells in me does His works. Believe me that I am in the Father and the Father

in me; or else believe me for the sake of the works them- ⨍
selves."[10] There was simply no way that Jesus could show
the Father separate from himself. We and God are one.
Again, we are not all of God's being, but we compose a
portion of God and are ourselves composed of God. This
is why the author of Genesis had to use the word
"Elohiym."

Some modern religious people do not like this concept and criticize it as a chief characteristic of the New
Age movement. The same criticism was leveled at Jesus
during His time. The religious authorities could not accept that any man was so closely connected with God. It
simply gave everyone their own direct line to God, requiring little of the authorities. But, as the Lord said in
Jeremiah, He does not want anyone between Him and
His created, no priest, no teachers. The Lord wants to
teach each one of us directly. As Jesus asked, "Why do
you get angry with me because I say that I am the Son of
God? Do not the scriptures say that you are gods?"

Obviously, we are not fully conscious of this, and
through this study we will discover why. Let's continue
with the nature of God and the Beginning.

THE DARK AND THE LIGHT

In ancient teachings, God is composed of two aspects,
a passive, impersonal quality and a dynamic, personal
quality. The Genesis verse, "darkness was upon the face
of the deep,"[11] refers to the first aspect of God. It is passive, quiet, impersonal, never changing and vast beyond
imagining. "The deep" is a beautiful term to use for this
aspect of God. Imagine what God's consciousness is like,
and then select words to describe it. I don't think we
could come up with a much better term than "the deep."
The Genesis author also associates it with "darkness."
But this is not in darkness in the sense of evil, rather in
the sense of unknown, unseen, unmanifested.

This line is then followed by, "the Spirit of God moved upon the face of the waters"[12] (no water had been created yet, so this may be interpreted as the waters of the deep, dark, infinite consciousness). The "Spirit of God," especially when it's moving, refers to a dynamic aspect of God. This is the Creator. It is personal, conscious, present, and knowable. It communicates with man throughout the scriptures.

This dynamic aspect of God says, "Let there be light,"[13] a metaphor for consciousness. It is the Logos. The light, or consciousness, was good, and was separated from the darkness, or unconsciousness. The darkness is subsequently called "Night," symbolizing the deep stillness of the unconscious. The light is called "Day,"[14] symbolizing the seen and the active. Following this pattern, an ancient Hebrew day began at sundown, recalling that darkness was before light, unconsciousness before consciousness, night before day, sleep before wakefulness.

When we are too much in the life of the Day, we are out of balance. Unconsciousness and the stillness of the Night are equally important to our health and well-being. Sleep, rest, the inward nature of prayer and meditation, and our stillness while listening are as important to us as wakefulness, activity, and speaking. This is expressed by the Psalmist as, "Day unto day pours forth speech, and night unto night reveals knowledge."[15] Our going in to our inner consciousness and our coming out to our outer consciousness is the balance of the inner places and unseen forces with the outer places and seen forces. We, as portions of God, are composed of both, and need to have these in balance.

SPIRIT

It's important that we understand "spirit" since it is key to our breakthrough. "Ruwach" is the Hebrew word used here. It literally means "wind," as in "the spirit

[wind] of God moved upon the face of the waters."[16] Wind is a poetic expression for the unseen force *behind* a manifested condition. We see the leaves and branches of a tree move and we know the unseen wind is the cause. As Jesus says to Nicodemus, "the wind blows where it will, and you hear the sound of it but do not know from where it comes or to where it goes; so is everyone who is born of the spirit."[17]

In Jesus' discussion with the woman at the well, He says, "God is Spirit, and those who worship Him must worship in spirit . . . "[18] The one, great Spirit is composed of our spirits, and true worship, or attunement, is achieved by "moving" into the spirit, as opposed to being predominantly conscious in the body and the mind. The disciple John begins his recording of the Revelation with, "I was in the spirit on the Lord's day . . . "[19] The Cayce discourses also speak to this important principle, "For the image in which man was created is spiritual, as He thy Maker is spiritual."[20]

Throughout the Old Testament, the *Spirit* of God brings two great gifts: *life* and *wisdom*. In Job, Elihu acknowledges that the Spirit has given life to us when he says, "the Spirit of God hath made me."[21] God's Spirit gives life to all, including minerals, plants, and animals. Where there is Spirit, there is life.

The Spirit's wisdom-giving power is expressed again by Elihu when he says to Job, "It is the spirit in a man, the breath of the Almighty, that makes him understand."[22] We also see how the spirit is known to bring wisdom when Pharaoh, after being astonished by Joseph's wisdom, asks his counsellors, "Can we find such a man as this, in whom is the spirit of God? Since God has shown you all this, there is none so discreet and wise as you are."[23] And in Jesus' hours before the crucifixion, He teaches that when He departs from the earth, the Holy Spirit will come and "teach you all things, and bring all things to your remembrance."[24] Where there is spirit, there is wisdom.

God, therefore, is collective, containing all and within all. It is unconscious and conscious. It is spirit and, as such, gives life and wisdom.

By the way, when I use the neutral pronoun "It" for God, it is because I simply cannot convey the correct impression of God by using either of the other two pronouns in our language, "he" or "she." God contains both the feminine and masculine. God is both Mother and Father. Further, God is not nearly so personal as the he/she pronouns imply. God is not *a person*, as we would think of a person. Therefore, "It" is, to my mind, the best pronoun. Of course, if I were true to the author of Genesis, I'd use "They," in keeping with the plural noun *Elohiym*. And though I truly believe "They" is an excellent pronoun for God, it does at times become awkward and tends to cause us to think of God as many, when God is one. "Hear, O Israel, the Lord thy God, the Lord is one."[25] Therefore, "It" will have to do.

Our Nature

SPIRIT AND SOUL

There is a subtle but significant distinction between *spirit* and *soul*. Spirit, as we have just reviewed, is associated with the wind, while soul corresponds to the breath. The spirit, like the wind, is *universal* and free; whereas the soul, like the breath, is more *individual* and contained. They are similar, both being air. As the wind moves by one's nostrils, it can be inhaled and become personal breath. In the first chapter of Genesis, we read that God created *adam* in Its image (Spirit). In chapter two, the "Lord God" (Yewah Elohiym) creates adam again by breathing the *breath* of life into him/her, and he becomes "a living being [soul]."[26] Notice how the "spirit [wind] of God" first created us in Its image, and later, we became living souls by the "breath" of the Lord God. Spirit is the wind; soul is the breath. One is more universal, the other is more individual. In the Cayce readings, the spirit is the life force, while the soul is that unique portion of each entity that is the sum total of all the entity has done with its gift of life. Soul is our unique story, our individualness.

Additionally, spirit is considered unchanging, whereas soul is developmental. The soul grows, learns, and becomes the companion to God. The spirit is the same yesterday, today, and tomorrow. It is life—eternal, unchanging life. Spirit is also considered the source of wisdom. When St. John says he is "in the spirit," he is referring to a process whereby he awakens to and attunes to the more spiritual aspect of his being; then, in turn, attunes that to the essence of all life, the Collective Spirit (Elohiym). Understanding this helps us break through to the spiritual.

FLESH

As we enter the earth realm, another quality is added to our composition—flesh. This adds blood to the metaphor of wind and breath. Now blood must permeate the lungs to get life from the breath, soul, which, in turn, gets its life from the wind, spirit.

Flesh (or our identification with it) is that portion of our being that separates us most from God. At one point during the great fall in Genesis, God says, "My spirit will not always be with man, for he is flesh."[27] God is not flesh. God is spirit. In order to fully know God, one must break through to the spirit. When "the great and terrible day of the Lord"[28] comes, it is terrible precisely because unspiritualized flesh will have little part in it. Those who have not regained some sense of their spiritual selves

will be in anguish over their fleshness. Jesus described it
to his disciples as, "weeping and gnashing of teeth."[29]
Let's review the story of creation, our beginnings.

OUR GENESIS

In the beginning God creates us in Its own image, "Let
us make man [adam] in *our* image, after *our* likeness . . .
So God created man [adam] in His own image, in the
image of God He created him; male and female He created them."[30] In this verse the Hebrew word for man is
"adam." This word is often translated as "reddish" or
"ruddy," but it also means "persons" or "people" collectively, and can mean an "indefinite someone." It is important to note in this verse that adam is male and
female in one, androgynous. It is not until later when the
"Lord God" creates adam "out of the dust of the earth,"
in other words, *in the flesh,* that these parts are separated. When this occurs, the name "adam" takes on the
meaning we most commonly associate with this word,
"ruddy" or "red," resulting from the blood in flesh.

It is important to realize that adam was first made in
the image of God, which we know is not flesh, but spirit,
female and male in oneness, unconscious and conscious
united. Then, symbolized by the changing of the name
of the creator from "God" to "Lord God" and, subsequently, to simply "Lord," we see the descent from direct
God-consciousness to self-consciousness.[31] This is the
descent from pure spirit to spiritualized flesh to disconnected flesh, at which time death takes hold. Understanding this helps us breakthrough to the original
consciousness and condition.

Another important point about this creation is that it
is a *group* creation, not just the creation of one famous
person. "Adam" at this stage of the creation is referring
to an original group of souls created by God in God's image, and subsequently made in spiritualized flesh by the

Lord God, then into mortal flesh by the Lord. According to the Cayce readings, the souls, those godlings within the One God, entered the earth in five places, five nations, five races; in one, they were called "Adam," and this is the story of those souls.[32]

At this point in Genesis, God has created everything in thought, in the mind of God, but not physically—all existed in God's consciousness. This is symbolized in the passage that comes *after* the seven days of creation: "Now no shrub of the field was yet in the earth [physically], and no plant of the field had yet sprouted, for the Lord God [note the name change] had not sent rain upon the earth; and there was no man [in flesh] to cultivate the ground."[33] Yet, we know the heaven, earth, and Adam had been created. The author is trying to convey to us that they had been created only in the mind of God not in form.

The original creation occurred *in God's infinite consciousness*. This was our natural home before entering the flesh. It is what is spoken of in Jesus' prayer to God, "And now, glorify Thou me together with Thyself, Father, with the glory which I had with Thee *before the world was*."[34] It is that realm spoken of when Jesus says to us, "I go to prepare a place for you . . . that where I am there you may be also. And you know the way where I am going."[35] Now, like many of us who are so much into physical consciousness, the disciple Thomas challenges this statement, "Lord, we do not know where you are going. How do we know the way?" But we do know the way. Deep within us is our true nature. Deep within us we remember the original home, and we know the way. Each of us was there in the beginning. Each of us was originally created in the image and likeness of God. Within us that original nature lives and intuitively knows its way home. As Jesus said, "No one ascend to heaven but he who has already descended from it, even the Son of Man."

FEMALE AND MALE

As we touched on earlier, ancient teachings hold that the One is composed of two aspects: that of the *dark*—meaning unseen, deep, and from out of which comes the other aspect, *light*—meaning seen, present and active. In the Eastern philosophies the terms "yin" and "yang" are used to express these characteristics. Yin is a feminine principle, yang a masculine one.

If we simply look objectively at the physical bodies of a female and male (the ultimate manifestation of these two aspects), we see the reflection of their innate qualities. A female's sexual organs are deep *within* her torso, a male's outside his. A female body has more *inner* processes than a male, such as menstrual cycles, conception, gestation, and milk production. The female reflects the characteristics of the inner aspect of God. Thus she is a reflection of the dark, unknown, unseen, unmanifested God, the yin. She represents the unconscious, sleep, and "Night" in Genesis, thus, "the Moon and the Stars." This would also imply that the feminine is the wind, the spirit, especially since she is the conceiver, the "life-giver."[36] On the other side, the male reflects the characteristics of the outer, manifested God. Thus, he is a reflection of the active, changing, personal, present God. He represents the conscious, wakefulness; "Day" in Genesis, thus the Sun. He is the "tiller of the soil," the doer, the conqueror. This would also imply that he is then the reflection of the breath, the soul, especially since he is the changing, developing "doer." Our original nature was composed of both these aspects in one being, but soon these were to be separated.

THE SEPARATION OF THE SEXES

Our fall from the original place of being is allegorically presented as the separation of the sexes and the eating of the "Fruit of the Tree of the Knowledge of Good and

Evil,"[37] which symbolizes consuming knowledge without understanding. The Cayce readings state it this way, " . . . seek not for knowledge alone. For, look—LOOK— what it brought Eve. Look rather for that wisdom which was eventually founded in she [Mary] that was addressed as 'the handmaid of the Lord' . . . "[38]

Because of our continued pull toward self-consciousness, we lose God-consciousness and *descend* into the narrow realm of the physical world. In Genesis 2:7, not God, but the "Lord God" creates us again, *after* the seven days of creation. This time we are created in spiritualized, physical form. "Then the Lord God formed man [adam, still male and female in one] of dust from the ground, and breathed into his nostrils the breath of life; and man became a living being [physically]."[39]

The author of Genesis tells us that now that man became flesh, he/she was so separated from the spiritual realm and God, that he/she was lonely. As the Lord God observes, "It is not good that the man [adam] should be alone; I shall make him a helper fit for him."[40] Lord God brought all the creatures of the earth before Adam, but there was none found companionable with this god-man in flesh. We were truly out of our natural element; as Jesus said, we are "not of this world."[41] But, having made the descent from heaven, we now had to find a better way to live in the physical realm.

Therefore, the Lord God caused a deep sleep to fall upon the androgynous man, and while he slept took one of his ribs[42] and closed up its place with flesh; and the rib which the Lord God had taken from the man he made into a woman and brought her to the man. Then the man said, "This at last is bone of my bones and flesh of my flesh; she shall be called Woman, because she was taken out of Man."[43]

In this deep sleep, the Lord God went into the inner places of the god-man and separated the two parts, bringing out one side of the whole being. These two sides could now be true help-mates one to the other. In Adam's poetic verse, the word "Man" is no longer "adam" but "ish," meaning male. The word "Woman" is "ishshah," meaning female. They that were one in "adam" are now separated into "ish" and "ishshah," man and woman. The male retained the name "Adam" and the female was called "Chavvah," meaning "life-giver." Eventually, she was named "Eve," meaning "mother of all."

As the great psychologist Carl Jung noted, we are only expressions of part of ourselves. If we project the masculine, then the feminine is in the unconscious. If we project the feminine, then the masculine is in the unconscious. To be whole, we must all get in touch with our other portion.

SEPARATION FROM GOD

In the beginning, adam represented the spirit-soul entity. This entity was, and remains, that portion of our being that is the companion to God. It is both male and female, and is in the image of God. We were composed of spirit (God), individualness (soul), and free will (the gift of God). However, as we children of God used free will to experience the infinite realms of the Cosmos, we became increasingly self-conscious, losing much of our God-consciousness. Eventually, some of us, not all, descended into the earth, the third dimension, and entered flesh. This required that we be made again in the flesh. Thus, we were formed out of the dust of the earth and our twin aspects were divided into yin and yang, male and female. We were naked, but at first our nakedness was not known to us and the Lord God did not call it our attention.[44]

THE FALL

The Lord God had commanded adam not to eat from

the Tree of the Knowledge of Good and Evil, saying "for in the day you eat from it, you shall surely die."[45] Up to this point, we were immortal beings, in the image of the immortal God. However, the further we moved from consciousness of our connectedness with the Eternal One, the more we lost connectedness to the source of Life. Adam and Eve began to live too completely in the flesh, losing touch with the life-giving Spirit. They began to reverse the flow of the Life Force, the élan vital, bringing it further into self-consciousness. This became so acute that, according to the Cayce readings, we actually experienced a death of the spirit.[46] To put it another way, we died to the spiritual influence.

Another significant piece to this puzzling death was the growth of something *other than God.*

SELF AND THE SERPENT

The serpent in the Garden represents SELF. It is self without regard for the Whole or for other beings. It is the self that seeks self-gratification, self-glorification, self-aggrandizement, self-centeredness. But in order for the potential companions of God to be true companions, they had to have a strong sense of self. As the Cayce readings state it: "That he may know himself to be himself and yet one with the Father [the Creator]."[47] Therefore, despite the dangers inherent in the development of self-consciousness, it was allowed because it was and remains the way to full realization of our role as divine companions. Yet, it often becomes a stumbling block.

The serpent, "more subtle than any other creature the Lord God had made,"[48] symbolizes two aspects of our being: 1) the life force, the kundalini; and, 2) the self (especially when it is not cooperating with the Whole).

In the Garden, our selfness (the serpent) convinces the two other aspects of our consciousness (Adam and Eve) that they could safely ignore God's guidance, and would *not* die, as God had stated. This resulted, though, in a further turning of consciousness and, with it, the life force was moved downward and outward—symbolized by the serpent's coming out of the tree and crawling on the ground.

Adam, Eve, and the serpent (all aspects of ourselves) fall from grace and lose the comfort of the garden. The Tree of Life, symbolizing immortality, is now protected from us, so we don't become eternal *terrestrial* beings when we are meant to be eternal *celestial* beings. Now we enter the cycle of life and death.

This is further symbolized in Eve's conception of two beings: Cain and Able. Cain literally means the "acquired" one (our forming egos). Abel means "a breath," or soul (our spiritually aware selves).[49] Of course, God favors the offerings of our souls more than our egos, as symbolized in Abel's offering as opposed to Cain's. However, Cain (ego) is angered by this and kills Abel (soul). Yet, when the Lord comes to Cain, He says, "Why are you angry, and why has your countenance fallen? If you do well, will you not be accepted? And if you do not do well, sin is couching at the door [of your consciousness]; its desire is for you, but you must master it."[50]

This is the great call to us. Yes, self-consciousness is dangerous. It may lead to self-centeredness and loss of union with the Whole. But it is such a wonderful gift that it is worth the trials. We simply must, as the Lord God said in the Garden, "Subdue the earth [i.e., our self-centered urges]."[51] As the Lord said to our Cain-self, "You must master it (self will)." By gaining control over this powerful gift, we will come to know ourselves to be ourselves and yet one with the Whole.

Stages to Regaining God-Consciousness

Thus, as ye take hold of the thought of God Consciousness, it may be just as pregnant a concept in mind as a baby in our body.[52]

In order to identify the stages of resurrection or rebirth in the spirit, let's enumerate the stages of our fall, and see how they can be turned around to bring resurrection. There are three major changes that brought on our loss of God-consciousness and all three can be turned around to regain it.

1) The death of the influence of the Elohiym Spirit and the rise of self.
2) The reverse of the flow of the Life Force.
3) The witness against us.

Let's examine these in detail.

1. We died to the spirit and gave birth to the self. The spirit and the universal consciousness of God is the true source and nature of Life, so when we died to it, we lost immortality and wisdom. Since God is spirit, we also lost consciousness of God. This is symbolized by the name changes for God and by our being denied access to the Tree of Life.[53] We became mortal. We also began to develop an even stronger sense of self, to the point that we lost awareness of self's connectedness to the Whole— God and other souls. This mounting sense of self separated us from direct contact with God, and is symbolized by our emergence into a single physical body, with singular gender. What was collective and united is now singular and separated. In order to regain God-consciousness, this movement from the spirit to the self must be turned around.

Jesus says to Nicodemus, "Unless one is born anew,

he cannot see the kindgom of God . . . That which is born of the flesh is flesh, and that which is born of the Spirit is spirit."[54] In this teaching we are given a great insight. We have been born of flesh and, using the old terms, that makes us "sons and daughters of man." However, we must also be born of the Spirit, making us "sons and daughters of God." During our physical lives, we should strive to experience the second birth, the birth of the spirit. This is spoken of and symbolized many times in both Testaments, beginning in the Garden itself. (Remember now, we are to consider physical activities as metaphors of what happens *within* consciousness. All the characters in these stories are also elements of our own soul development.)

At the time of the loss of the Garden, God prophesies that Eve, and all women after her, will give birth only through much effort and pain, but that her line will one day give birth to the Savior, to the One who will subdue (or reverse) the serpent's influence.[55] In our personal experience, that translates to this: our feminine, inner, deeper self—with all its unseen forces and spiritual powers—will conceive, gestate and deliver a new consciousness which will raise the serpent up, be "born anew," and regain what was lost. This will be our spiritual selves.

The story of Mary's conception and delivery of a new child is perhaps the fullest expression of this idea. Let's review the angel Gabriel's description of what will happen to her:

> Behold, you will conceive in your womb [the womb of our inner consciousness], and bear a child . . . He will be great, and will be called the Son of the Most High; and the Lord God will give Him the throne . . . and He will reign over the house of Jacob forever; and His kingdom will have no end." And Mary said to the angel,

"How can this be, since I am a virgin?" [From the earthly perspective, as a daughter of man, how can this be done? Almost the same reaction Nicodemus had to Jesus' teaching about spiritual birth.] The angel answered and said to her, "The Holy Spirit will come upon you, and the power of the Most High will overshadow you; and for that reason the holy offspring shall be called the son of God."[56]

The description of this conception is reminiscent of deep, meditative, mystical experience—"The Holy Spirit will come upon you, and the power of the Most High will overshadow you." It also calls to mind other wonderful expressions of this experience:

And it shall come to pass that I will *pour out my spirit upon all flesh*; and your sons and daughters shall prophesy, your old shall dream dreams, and your young shall see visions."[57]

... suddenly a sound came from heaven like the rush of a mighty wind [spirit], and it filled all the house where they were sitting. And there appeared to them tongues as of fire, distributed and resting on each one of them. And they were all *filled with the Holy Spirit* ... "[58]

How precious is thy steadfast love, O God! The children of men take refuge in the shadow of thy wings. They feast on the abundance of thy inner place, and thou givest them drink from the river of thy delights. For within thee is the fountain of life; in thy light do we see light."[59]

Another important expression of this idea comes as Jesus nears the end of his physical ministry. At the last Passover dinner, Jesus says that his soul has become troubled.[60] Later, as He sought to calm the troubled spirits of His disciples—they were beginning to realize He would soon be leaving them—He compared their feelings to those of a woman in labor: She has sorrow because her hour of pain and struggle are upon her, but when she is delivered of the child, she no longer remembers the anguish, for the joy that a child is born.[61]

So it is with us in our hour of delivery of our spiritual child. Each of us has conceived this spiritual being within our hearts and minds. We have nourished it in the wombs of our consciousnesses. Now it is time for us to deliver it, and the pain and struggle of this is upon us. However, once delivered of it, we will rejoice that a child is born—not a child of man, but a child of God. Our spirit will be *present*, and will be able to attune to God directly, which is the purpose of spiritual breakthrough.

In the Revelation we also see a woman in labor, a heavenly woman:

> And a great portent appeared in heaven, a woman clothed with the Sun, with the Moon under her feet, and on her head a crown of twelve stars; she was with child and she cried out in her pangs of birth, in anguish for delivery."[62]

She, as well as Mary, symbolizes the fulfillment of God's promise to Eve. Out of her will come the savior, who will overcome selfishness and reunite us with the Whole. Like Mary, she also represents for us the process of spiritual breakthrough.

We have already *conceived* our redeemer, our messiah, our *spiritual* being within our hearts and minds—or we wouldn't even be studying these things. Now we must fully realize it by giving birth to it, letting it become fully alive and present. This requires that we lay down our outer selves and give birth to our inner selves. We must subjugate the flesh, the earthly portion of our being, to the Higher Forces, and give place or space in our consciousness and life for our reborn spiritual being. As Jesus expresses it, "Unless a grain of wheat falls into the earth and dies, it remains alone; but if it dies, it bears much fruit. He who loves his life loses it, and he who hates his life in this world will keep it for eternal life."[63]

We must yield to the will of the spirit within us, allowing it to have expression in our lives. If we will seek its way more than our own, eventually it will be fully manifest. We will be, once again, spiritual beings, even while in the physical world. As Jesus states it, "When you have lifted up the son of man, then you will know . . . "[64] When we have raised our earthly selves to the level of consciousness of our heavenly selves, then we will know what it's all about and who we really are.

2. *We reversed the flow of the Life Force.* Our kundalini energy was used to physically manifest and breed. It flows down our spines and out to the world, mostly in gratification and self-exaltation. This is, literally, the fall of the serpent.

Moses (symbolizing one "drawn out"[65] of the unconscious) leads the seekers out of material captivity (symbolized by Egypt) and away from the control of Pharaoh (symbolic of the ego self), across the wilderness to the Mount of God, where we reconnect with God and eventually enter the Promised Land.[66] One of the great signs that Moses performs, following God's guidance, is to raise the serpent, and all who look upon it are healed from its bite.[67] While teaching Nicodemus about "heavenly things," Jesus refers to this great sign saying, "No one has ascended into heaven but he who descended from heaven, even the Son of man. And as Moses lifted up the serpent in the wilderness, even so must the Son of man be lifted up, that whoever believes may in Him have eternal life."[68] If we interpret this teaching for us as individuals, it shows that through misuse of the life-force (kundalini, serpent power) and self-consciousness (the serpent, dragon, Satan, etc.), we descended from heaven and lost consciousness of our nature as sons and daughters of God, believing ourselves to be no more than sons and daughters of other humans. If we wish to ascend to heaven and regain our heritage as children of God, then we must raise the life-force (raise the serpent) and raise the consciousness of our physical selves (raise the son of man) so that we may once again have the glory that was ours before the world was, and live eternally with God.

3. We are a witness against ourselves. Our conscience knows what we have done. The resulting guilt, self-condemnation, and self-doubt holds us from fully entering into God's all-knowing presence. This is expressed in the story of Job. Let's take a moment to review key parts of this story.

The story of Job begins, "Now there was a day when the sons [and daughters] of God came to present themselves before the Lord, and Satan also came among them."[69] As a result of our movement into selfness and the flesh, we are not able to come into the presence of God, even though we are "the sons [and daughters] of God." We therefore present ourselves to "the Lord" (the Hebrew is "Yahweh"). Even then, because of our changes, when we come before the Lord, we bring Satan with us. Satan here symbolizes our growing self-centered nature, in opposition to God and the Collective. Literally, the name Satan means "the accuser." The Lord asks Satan, our selfness, "Have you considered my servant Job, that there is none like him on the earth, a blameless and upright man, who fears God and turns away from evil?"[70] Our selfness then witnesses against the goodness symbolized in Job, saying that if the Lord puts forth His hand and touches anything of Job's possessions or Job's flesh, he will curse the Lord to His face. Is Job righteous because his physical life is comfortable, or is he righteous because he loves God, loves the spirit, more than the temporary pleasures of the physical, self-centered life? The Lord tells Satan to test him. Satan tries Job terribly, but Job does not curse the Lord for his physical pain and loss. Job's friends also accuse him of sin, since otherwise these bad things would not have come upon him and his family. But Job searches his heart and finds no evil in himself. Then, Job crys to the Lord and the Lord comes to him. They engage in a dynamic conversation, coming to know one another directly. All that Job lost is restored a hundredfold. But, better than that, Job has come to know the Lord directly, and the Lord has come to know Job.

Satan, our self-centered selves, is a witness against us. When we come before the Lord, the all-knowing consciousness, we bring this accuser with us.

Another example of this is found in the Old Testament Book of Zechariah, when Joshua is presented to the Lord. " . . . Joshua the high priest standing before the angel of the Lord, and Satan standing at his right hand to *accuse* him. And the Lord said to Satan, 'The Lord rebuke you, O Satan! The Lord who has chosen Jerusalem rebuke you! Is not this a brand plucked from the fire?' Now Joshua was standing before the angel, clothed with filthy garments, and the angel said to those who were standing before him, 'Remove the filthy garments from him.' And to him he said, 'Behold, *I have taken your iniquity away* from you, and I will clothe you with festal robes.'"[71] Later, the Lord says, "I will remove the guilt of this land in a single day."[72] And a little later, the Lord says this is accomplished "not by might, nor by power, but by my Spirit."[73] The garments of our consciousness are soiled from our self-centered activities and thoughts, but the spirit can and will cleanse them in a moment, and rebuke the accuser in our minds.

Perhaps the clearest example of the need to rid our consciousness of the accuser is found in the Revelation. The Revelation is more than a book of prophecy; it is an insight into the very nature of our *inner* passage into full God-consciousness. As the Cayce readings put it: "The Revelation . . . is a description of . . . thy own consciousness . . . "[74] "Why, then, is it presented, ye ask, in the form of symbols? These are for those that were, or will be, or may become, through the seeking, those initiated into an understanding of the glories that may be theirs if they will but put into work, into activity, that they know in the present . . . These [the symbols] represent self; self's body-physical, self's body-mental, self's body-spiritual . . . "[75]

Earlier in this study, a scene from the Revelation was described in which the divine pregnant woman is striving to be delivered of her heavenly baby. Swirling about her is a red dragon.[76] This dragon is the full grown serpent of the Garden, Satan, the accuser.[77] It is the self-seeking aspect of our being. It is ready to devour our new consciousness in a belly of self-doubt and self-condemnation. But the archangel Michael, the Lord and Protector of the Way (also an aspect of our being), fights with this dragon and drives it out of heaven, out of our higher consciousness. Then, a loud voice from heaven (our higher consciousness) cries out,

> Now the salvation and the power and the kingdom of our God and the authority of his Anointed One have come, for the accuser of our brethren has been thrown down, who ac-

cuses them day and night before our God. And
they have conquered him by the blood of the
Lamb and by the word of their testimony, for
they loved not their lives even unto death. Rejoice then, O heaven and you that dwell therein!
But woe to you, O earth and sea, for the devil
has come down to you in great wrath, because
he knows that his time is short!"[78]

We must drive out of our minds this accuser, this self-
doubt, this self-condemning influence, if we are to fully
regain God-consciousness. Our consciousness will rejoice when it is done, for now our divine feminine can
safely deliver our spiritual nature.

Jesus and God-Consciousness

The life of Jesus connects deeply with these stages in
the regaining of God-consciousness, and it wouldn't be
going too far to say that he *initiated* them.

Perhaps the main contribution of his life was to serve
as the *pattern* for being connected with God-consciousness. Having lost that connection ourselves, we were
very weak in the area of spirit, but growing strong in the
areas of the physical and the mental. We needed help
regaining the spiritual influences and consciousness.
Cayce puts it this way:

> One finds self a body, a mind, a soul; each
> with its own attributes and its activity in the
> earth. An entity, then, is a pattern of that which
> is also a spiritual fact; Father, Son, Holy Spirit.
> These are one, just as an individual entity is
> one. An entity, then, is the pattern of divinity
> in materiality, or in the earth. As man found

> himself out of touch with that complete con-
> sciousness of the oneness of God, it became
> necessary that the will of God, the Father, be
> made manifested, that a pattern be introduced
> into man's consciousness. Thus the son of man
> came into the earth . . . "[79]

Jesus taught us much about the *way of spirit* in re-
sponding to others and to situations that arise. In rela-
tion to casting out the witness against us, He showed us
that to be free of that influence, we need only *cease doing any accusing ourselves.* Coming into a society that
held only negative feelings towards lepers, prostitutes,
foreign soldiers, and tax-collectors, He accepted and
loved them all. He showed us that *the way of spirit* lies
not in trying to eliminate in ourselves (and others!)
whatever the accuser might point to. Instead, He taught
us to *love* one another and ourselves and to subdue the
accuser's voice of condemning judgment.

Even at the end of his life, Jesus was teaching us about
strengthening our connection with spirit. The crucifixion is symbolic of much more than restitution for sin. In
its deepest meaning it is the way to resurrection. Let's
take a closer look at the significant activities and discus-
sions leading up to and following the crucifixion.

It begins at the Last Supper. That Passover night and
meal has its origins in ancient Egypt on the night the
Angel of Death came upon all incarnate beings in Egypt,
exempting only those who had the blood of the lamb
upon the doorpost of their house[80] (symbolic of the
doorpost of their consciousness). This freed the seekers
from bondage to the ruler of Earth, allowing them to go
to the Mount of God and the Promised Land.

So, now, Jesus and His disciples relive this moment,
breaking bread and sharing wine together—*symbols* of
breaking flesh and shedding blood. As the evening un-

folds, Jesus becomes troubled. He says, "And now my soul is troubled because my hour has come upon me. And what should I do? Call to my Father in heaven and ask Him to deliver me from this hour? No, for this hour have I come."[81] Yet, a few hours later in the garden He is troubled again, "My soul is very sorrowful, even to death ... Abba (literally, "Papa"), Father, all things are possible to Thee; remove this cup from me; yet not what I will, but what Thou wilt."[82] This is the outer man wrestling with the great transition from self-determined, physical man to God-centered, spiritual man. The physical, outer, earthy self does not inherit the kingdom of heaven.[83] The spiritual, inner, heavenly self inherits the kingdom. Thus, the deep meaning behind the ancient Hebrew concept of the blood-sacrifice relates directly to the subjugation of flesh to the spirit. Breaking through the flesh encasement (shedding the blood) yields the spirit and gives it its rightful place as the dominant, true self. As the process is completed, the physical self cries, "Why hast Thou foresaken me?"[84] But the intuitive soul says, "Into thy hands I commend my spirit,"[85] and gives up the flesh life for the spirit life. Now we enter into the tomb, the cave, the coffin—death, sleep and the dark unconscious. Then, by the unseen powers of the Spirit, we rise again, reborn. Only now we are predominantly spiritual beings manifesting physically, rather than physical beings with spiritual attributes.

As Job was restored a hundredfold, as Jesus came again to eat fish and honey with His disciples on the beach after His resurrection, and all that was lost in the Genesis Garden was regained in the "new heaven and new earth"[86] of the Revelation. So will we be restored. The Tree of Life, the Water of Life, and the new dwelling will be given to us to "take freely."[87]

In the ancient Egyptian temple of the Great Pyramid, the coffin in the upper chamber is empty. In Jerusalem when the women came to anoint Jesus' body, they found that the tomb held no decaying body. All initiates of the ancient mystery schools were taught *there is no death.* That is, there is no death when the Spirit is present and predominant.

When we lay aside our personal, earthly, physical interests—even though we feel "forsaken"—and commend ourselves into God's hands (the Spirit's life-giving and wisdom-giving power), we rise up again, a new person, one with God, God-conscious again—fully integrating body, mind, soul, and spirit and attuning them to the Great Spirit, the Elohiym, God. Now what was separated is rejoined. What was lost is found. What was dead is alive. This is spiritual breakthrough.

> Dost thou seek to enter into the glories of the Father? Whosoever will may come, may take of the water of life freely—even as flows from the throne of the Lamb. . . . If ye will accept, the blood cleanses from all unrighteousness. Saves self from what? To what are ye called? To know that only from the falling away of self may ye be saved—unto the glorifying of self in Him may ye be saved.
>
> Then, whosoever will, come!"[88]

2

MEETING GOD—FACE TO FACE

The Mount of God

Our bodies are the temples of the Living God. The way to spiritual breakthrough is found in God's teachings from the Mount to Moses and the people. One of the first teachings was to build a new temple, a portable one, with an outer court, inner court, holy place and a holy of holies. In this temple God promised to meet them, face to face. This temple represented what would eventually be understood as the human body and mind. The outer court (the physical body), the inner court (the spiritual man) is approached through the mental body (the holy place) and on to the holy of holies, where the Father/Mother may speak as though face to face.

Another major mount experience comes when Jesus

ascends the Mount with his three disciples and is transfigured. In this vision on the Mount, the law and prophets were represented in the physical, the mental, the spiritual: in Moses (physical), Elijah (mental), and the Christ (spiritual). Recall that during the transfiguration the disciples saw Moses and Elijah with the transfigured Jesus. Each represented an aspect of the path or way to spiritual breakthrough. Moses led the way out from the lower self's control (symbolized by Pharaoh and the captivity in Egypt). Moses then struggled through the desert to the Mount of God where he learned from God directly, face to face. However, Moses ultimately could not enter the Promised Land, as the physical self does not inherit the Kingdom. Therefore, the mental self (symbolized by Elijah) seeks God throughout the earth but does not find Him in the earth; not in the lightning, earthquake, fire or wind. It is not until he backs up to the mouth of the cave (enters within his deeper consciousness) and hears "a still, small voice" within his own head that God comes fully into his consciousness. Finally, the spiritual seeker through the Immanuel experience (God among man) realizes the flesh and the mind as filled with the Holy Spirit. Human and Divine are one, consciously one, face to face.

"For the body is indeed the temple of the living God, and He has promised to meet thee there, in the holy of holies, in the Mount within." says reading 1152-2. And in 882-1, "'There I shall meet thee, in the Mount of thyself.' For thy body indeed is the temple of the living God; there He may meet thee as ye turn within. There ye may find the greater understanding; for He hath not left His children empty-handed; for He has prepared the way."

Meditation, deep meditation, is one of the primary means by which we make contact and begin the transfiguration process. In reading 707-6 we have, "Rememberest thou all that has been given as to the manner in which the individual finds self? Did Moses receive direction other than by the period in the Mount? Did Samuel receive other than by meditating within his own closet? Did David not find more in meditating within the valley and the cave? Did not the Master in the Mount and in the garden receive the answers of those directing forces?" "Why, ye may ask, did the Master love to be in Galilee when the house of the Lord His God was in Jerusalem? Why did He love to be alone in the Mount?" [3357-2]

Going to the Mount of God, which is ultimately within us, is the manner by which we find God-consciousness. It is not simply silent meditation, but is an *ascending* meditation, as going *up* on the Mount implies. Spiritual Breakthrough requires that we raise ourselves into the Universal Consciousness and the Great Spirit.

Here is a fascinating vision into that original experience on the Holy Mount, Cayce describes it in his reading 440-16: "They had seen the Lord Jehovah descend into the Mount, they had seen the Mount so electrified by the presence of the od of the people and ohm of the Omnipotent to such an extent that no living thing could remain in the Mount or on same, save those two [Moses & Joshua] who had been cleansed by their pouring out of themselves to God, in the cleansing of their bodies, in the cleansing of their minds." Cayce's reference to the "od of the people" refers to a term coined by Reichenbach (1788-1869) to explain an unseen force in nature that manifests itself in magnetism, hypnotism and light, called the "odic force." "Od" is most likely derived from the Greek word *hodos* which means path or way, and is used in such modern electrical words as anode and cathode. Cayce's use of the word "Ohm" is most probably referring to the term coined by one of Reichenbach's contemporaries, Georg Simon Ohm (1789-1854). This term is a measurement of electrical resistance. However, the way Cayce uses the term in the readings is not like this at all. He is clearly equating the ohm force directly with electricity. Therefore, we could translate this Mount experience as, "the magnetism of the people's hearts and minds seeking God so long and so hard had attracted the Omnipotent to descend upon the Mount, and It brought with It the powers of the Omnipotent, powers which destroy as well as enlighten (the Ohm of electricity)."

In meditation, the Mount is equated with the sixth spiritual center of the body, and the Holy of Holies with the seventh.

Meditation: A Way to God

We must be clear that meditation is an *altered state of consciousness.* It is not a method for getting our normal consciousness to feel better. "You don't have the meditation because . . . you want to feel better, but to attune self to the infinite!"[1] We must set our normal, everyday selves aside and allow our deeper, spiritual selves to attune to the Infinite. This is perhaps the most fundamental and yet the most difficult requirement of meditation. But it can be done. The body, mind, and soul are interconnected in such a way that certain actions will automatically lead to "the magic silence"[2] and the awakening of our better selves.

Actions That Lead Inward

We have two nervous systems. One (the Central Nervous System) we use mostly for our outer life—for acting consciously in the physical. The other (the Autonomic) governs those functions such as breathing and digestion that are taken care of without our conscious participation.

What do these two nervous systems have to do with successful meditation? When we quiet the outer system and do something to stimulate the inner system, we are setting aside our outer selves and actually activating our souls. For example, let's sit down and stop using our musculoskeletal systems. Let's reduce our sense-perception by closing down our five senses—close our eyes, stop touching, listening, smelling and tasting. This quiets the outer system and the outer self. Now, let's take hold of some part of the inner system that the soul has charge of and let's alter it. The most popular one is the breath. The autonomic system, under the control of the subconscious mind and soul, is in charge of and directly connected to the breath. If we start changing the breath, we cause the soul and subconscious mind to become alert to the changes. This is an action that leads from our outer selves to our inner selves, and ultimately to an altered state of consciousness.

Physical Changes

Now we know from the research done in the '70s with TM meditators and others, that the body goes through many changes during meditation. As researchers Wallace and Benson discovered, meditation causes measurable physical changes. "There is a reduction in oxygen consumption, carbon dioxide elimination and the rate and volume of respiration; a slight increase in the acidity of the arterial blood; a marked decrease in the blood-lactate level; a slowing of the heartbeat; a considerable increase in skin resistance; and an electroencephalogram pattern of intensification of slow alpha waves with occasional theta-wave activity."[3]

Reading 5752-3 expands on the wonderful changes: "Meditate . . . in the inner secrets of the consciousness, and the cells in the body become aware of the awakening of the life . . . " The cells of the body become aware? According to the readings, every cell in the body has consciousness, and that consciousness may be raised or lowered. The reading goes on, "In the mind, the cells of the mind become aware of the life in the spirit." The cells of the mind, life in the spirit? Interesting concepts, aren't they? "God is Spirit, and those who worship Him must do so in spirit . . . "4 Then, if raising the consciousness leads to awareness of "life in the spirit," it leads to life with God—the Great Spirit. The wonderful thing about this whole process is that we activate it by entering into the magic silence.

The Magic Silence

For those of you who are just beginning with meditation or who have always had trouble meditating, let me spend a moment to describe this very simple yet effective way to meditate. Then, as you progress with it, you can move on to Kundalini Meditation. The Magic Silence method is a simple yet powerful way for anyone to get into meditation—especially beginners and those who have difficulty meditating.

Using a combination of an affirmation and a mantra, coordinated with our breathing, we can enter into the magic silence. Let's use a modification of a line from Psalm 46 (recommended by the readings), "Be still and know God." In order to fully succeed with this affirmation/mantra, not only do we need the power of the words, we must also take hold of the breath and create a breathing pattern that arouses the soul. It works like this: "Be STILL" [inhale slowly while feeling the word "still" and then exhale slowly] "and know GOD" [inhale slowly while feeling the word "God" and then exhale slowly].

While you are saying the phrases, breathe normally. Keep the breath relaxed yet *under your control.*

If you are experiencing the feeling/breathing phase of this method as going well, and no distractions are occurring, then add a full breathing cycle before going on to the next phrase. If you are in the "stillness" or the "Godness" between the phrases, remain in it as long as your consciousness holds there, breathing gently and evenly. If your consciousness wanders, then bring it back by saying (in your mind) the next phrase. These silent periods in between the phrases are the more important parts of this practice. The phrases gather and direct the consciousness, but the spaces of silence are golden, or as the readings say, "magical." So, as long as you are silent and still, stay there; don't feel a need to move on to the next phrase or to continue repeating the phrases.

This method of combining an affirmation/mantra with breathing will bring even the weakest meditator into a deep stillness and a heightened sense of Godness.

To move deeper, add three "OM's" on the end of the last phrase: "Be STILL [feel and breathe], and know GOD [feel and breathe], OOOMMMM [feel and breathe] OOOMMMM [feel and breathe] OOOMMMM [feel and breathe]. This can be out loud in the beginning and then silently in your mind as you go deeper. When chanting the OM incantation aloud, remember that true chanting is an *inner sounding*, not an outer singing. Keep the sound resonating within the cavities of your body. Beginning with the abdominal cavity, rising to the pulmonary cavity and then on into the cranial cavity, let the sound carry you deeper.

I've taught this method to people who have never meditated before, had them in a deep silence for twenty minutes, and watched them coming out of it with that wonderful glaze in their eyes that results from an altered state. Their outer self is moved, yet uncertain as to exactly what has happened. But they know they have just meditated well. I've also had people who had tried meditation for years with little success come out of one of these sessions with the biggest smiles on their faces—victory at last!

Keys to This Method

There are three keys to this method. First, the power of the words "still" and "God," and their effect on us. Second, the connection between the breath and the soul—allowing us to arouse our souls by taking hold of the breathing pattern. Third, the spaces of silence between the words while breathing. These spaces grow longer and longer as one practices. Eventually, an hour's meditation is easy (and recommended in the readings). According to the readings, and many other sources, the silence is in itself transforming. One need not "do" or "hear" anything when in meditation. Abide in the silence and it works its magic.

Now I would like us to look at another area of the total meditation picture. I would not recommend going on to this next practice (kundalini meditation) until you have practiced the Magic Silence method with much success, and feel you are ready to go deeper. As with medicine so it is with meditation: one person's poison may be another's cure, and activities that may be harmful at one stage in life may be quite helpful at another. You have to judge what is best for you now, and continue to evaluate your readiness as you progress.

It may appear contradictory to say that silence is in itself transforming and then to describe another form of meditation in which inner activities are used to effect greater transformation, but such is the case with the Cayce readings, and other sources. The explanation for this is that the manifold nature of full enlightenment and transformation is such that contradiction and paradox are elements of *any* method. After all, we are dealing with celestial beings in terrestrial forms, spirits in flesh, gods who are also human, eternal beings in temporary manifestations. Paradox and contradiction are bound to be a part of any process that attempts to resolve or integrate these.

Furthermore, as we progress with our development, we naturally become more able to handle complexity and intricacy. We become more aware of and participate in the many aspects of the Godhead, the Universal Consciousness, with all its diversity.

Raising the Serpent

Not only Adam and Eve fell in the Garden, the serpent fell also. And, as Moses raised the serpent in the desert, so must we all raise the serpent power within ourselves in order to receive the presence and the power of God, the Omnipotent, within our temples, our bodies. One of the most primary practices for doing this is kundalini meditation.

Like the Magic Silence method, this method will use words, breath and spaces of silence, but in more powerful ways. Since there is more power involved, there are more warnings in the readings about using this method without proper preparation and self-examination.

Warnings

"But make haste SLOWLY! Prepare the body, prepare the mind, before ye attempt to loosen it in such measures or manners that it may be taken hold upon by those influences which constantly seek expressions of self rather than of a living, constructive influence of a CRUCIFIED Savior. Then, crucify desire in self; that ye may be awakened to the real abilities of helpfulness that lie within thy grasp . . . without preparation, desires of EVERY nature may become so accentuated as to destroy . . . "[5] Therefore, let's examine our purposes, searching our hearts for our true passion. Is it cooperation and co-ordination with God, or are we still longing to gratify some lingering desires of our own self interests?

The Taoist meditators of *The Secret of the Golden Flower* talk about the right method being like one wing of a bird, the other wing being the right *heart*. A wise seeker must remember, the bird cannot fly with only one wing. All seekers must have the right method *and* the right heart.

The Ideal

The right-heart concept leads us naturally to the readings' teaching that an ideal should be raised as we seek to awaken the life force. What is our ideal? To whom or what do we look for examples of better behavior, better choices, better uses for our energies, better relating skills with others? What standard guides us in conceiving our better selves? Who is the author of our "Book of Life?" Is it the circumstances of life? Is it our self-interests?

These are important questions from the perspective of the Cayce readings, questions that should be considered before going on with the powerful kundalini forces aroused in this method of meditation. As the readings say, we can build a Frankenstein or a god using basically the same meditative method. It all depends on the ideal held as the practice progresses.

FIND that which is to YOURSELF the more certain way to your consciousness of PURIFYING body and mind, before ye attempt to enter into the meditation as to raise the image of that through which ye are seeking to know the will or the activity of the Creative Forces; for ye are RAISING in meditation actual CREATION taking place within the inner self![6]

The readings would advise anyone who feels unable to "set the carnal aside" and attune to a high ideal for the period of meditation to *not* meditate—and instead to pray. If the prayer then changes you and you feel that you can set the carnal forces aside, you may enter into meditation. Otherwise, stay away from it. Meditation gives power to whatever is in the consciousness and desires of the person. Make sure these are pure and of the highest.

Jesus Christ

The Cayce readings present Jesus Christ as not only a high ideal but as a powerful force of protection for anyone seeking to loosen their life force, to open the bio-spiritual seals, and enter into the presence of God. Christ is presented as an *advocate* for us before the Godhead. To call on this protection and guidance is to call on the greatest resource available. However, the readings do not put the religion that formed around Jesus Christ above other religions. The readings are too universal for that. Seekers from any religious faith can use the power of Christ in their meditative practice and still remain loyal to their religion. Here's an example of this perspective, from reading 281-13:

If there has been set the mark (mark meaning here the image that is raised by the individual in its imaginative and impulse force)
such that it takes the form of the ideal the individual is holding as its standard to be raised to,
... *then* the individual (or the image) bears the
mark of the Lamb, or the Christ, or the Holy
One, or the Son, or any of the names we may
have given to that which *enables* the individual
to enter THROUGH IT into the very presence
of that which is the creative force from within
itself—see? ...
Raising then in the inner self that image of
the Christ, love of God-Consciousness, is *making* the body so cleansed as to be barred
against all powers that would in any manner
hinder.

Notice how "Christ" is given as equivalent to the "love
of God-Consciousness." Seekers from *any* religion may
have love of God-Consciousness. Christ in this perspective is more universal than the religion that possesses
that name. Notice also how "love of God-Consciousness"
cleanses us of self-interests that may hinder or harm us.

However, there is much more to this reading than
ecumenism and protection. Cayce is giving us a great
insight into just how a meditator may be transported
from a good meditative stillness into the very presence
of the Creative Force, God—with all the ramifications of
such an experience. If in our imaginative forces we can
conceive or form the ideal (the standard) to which we
seek to be raised, then we (as the Revelation states) bear
the mark or the sign of that power (whatever name we
give it) that enables us to enter *through it* into the very
presence of God within us, the Creative Force within us.
Despite the power of some of the other techniques in

this form of meditation, imaging the ideal is seminal to transformation. Reading 1458-1 points out our only limitation: "The entity is only limited to that it sets as its ideal." We are "gods in the making" if we can conceive ourselves to be such—in cooperation and coordination with the Great God.

The Kundalini and Eternal Life

As we have seen, the readings interweave Judeo-Christian teachings found throughout the Old and New Testaments, but particularly in the book of The Revelation, with concepts and practices from ancient Hinduism and Yoga. The fundamental concepts are these: The kundalini is metaphorically seen as the great serpent power fallen from its original place of honor. As Adam and Eve fell from grace in the Garden, so did the serpent. But as Moses raised the serpent in the desert and Jesus raised it to life everlasting,[7] so each of us must raise our serpent power to its rightful, original place of honor. Kundalini meditation is intended to do just that.

This kundalini or life force is *within* the human body, the temple. Normally it is used in ways that dissipate it, eventually leading to aging and death of the body. All people are allowed to use their life force as they choose (at least within the parameters of their karma). Whether they dissipate it consciously or unconsciously makes no difference. When it's gone, it's gone. But it doesn't have to be this way. As the readings put it, " . . . if there will be gained that consciousness, there need not be ever the necessity of a physical organism aging . . . seeing this, feeling this, knowing this, ye will find that not only does the body become revivified, but by the creating in every atom of its being the knowledge of the activity of this Creative Force . . . spirit, mind, body [are] renewed."[8]

The "elan vital" of the Western world and the "kundalini" of the Eastern world follows natural laws, and can be made to flow in rejuvenative ways which enhance and extend the life. This is not only possible with kundalini meditation, but it is a valuable goal to pursue. Here's one reading's statement on this: "How is the way shown by the Master? What is the promise in Him? The last to be overcome is death. Death of what? The *soul* cannot die, for it is of God. The body may be revivified, rejuvenated. And it is to that end it may, the body, *transcend* the earth and its influence."[9] This meditation practice works directly with the forces of life.

Prayer Words

Now let's look at the mechanics of this method. Assuming that our ideals, purposes and hearts are in the right place, that we have crucified our selfish desires, conceived of our ideal, and drawn on the power and protection of the Christ, "love of God-Consciousness"—let's begin with *prayer-words for the seven chakras.* (the spiritual centers of the body). These words vary with different practices, but the Cayce readings teach that one reason the Master created the Lord's Prayer was for this purpose.[10] The readings give a slightly different version of the prayer, which we'll use.[11] The readings are also comfortable with the feminine aspect of the Godhead as well as the masculine, so let's also use this. As you say the prayer, feel the *meaning* of the words as your consciousness is directed to the location of the chakra.

Edgar Cayce's Vision of the Lord's Prayer & the Spiritual Centers of the Body	
Prayer/**Key Word**	Order/Gland/Center
Our Father/Mother which art in	
Heaven	7th/Pituitary/Third Eye
hallowed be thy	
Name	6th/Pineal/Crown
Thy kingdom come, thy	
Will	5th/Thyroid/Throat
be done; in **Heaven**, so in **Earth**.	(Heaven represents the three upper centers, earth the four lower ones.)
Give us for tomorrow the	
Bodily Needs	1st/Ovaries-Testes/ Root
And forgive us our	
Trespasses	3rd/Adrenals/Solar Plexus
as we forgive those who have and do trespass against us. And be thou the	
Guide	2nd/Leydig/Lyden ("the seat of the soul")
in the times of turmoil, temptation, and trouble; leading us through paths of	
Righteousness—	4th/Thymus/Heart
right heart, right attitude, right purposes; for Thy	
Name's sake.	6th/Pineal/Crown

To fully realize the power of this prayer, one must understand that it is intended to call forth the highest in each chakra. Just as we felt the words "stillness" and "God" in the earlier affirmation/mantra, so now we must feel or imagine *the change* brought on by these words and their meanings. Take your time. Consider this as part of the meditation period.

The order of the chakra prayer is significant in that it attempts to awaken the higher chakras *before* awakening the lower ones. This is the best approach. Awakening the first chakra before the seventh and sixth is like opening the serpent basket without the charm of the flute. The serpent is loose to its own interests, rather than under the charm of the higher music. Keep a higher ideal, a higher purpose, a right heart, and the consciousness focused predominantly on the higher centers. Draw the kundalini upward.

BREATH POWER

Now once again we take hold of the breath. This time we take a stronger hold and use it in ways that arouse the life force and draw it up through the chakras of this wonderful bio-spiritual instrument in which we abide. Why the breath? "BREATH is the basis of the living organism's activity . . . this opening of the centers or the raising of the life force may be brought about by certain characters of breathing—for, as indicated, the breath is power in itself; and this power may be directed . . ."[12]

STRENGTHENING AND OPENING BREATH

There are several breathing patterns we may use. The first is described often in the readings. It begins with a deep inhalation through the right nostril, filling the lungs and feeling *strength*! Then exhalation through the mouth. This should be felt throughout the torso of the body—STRENGTH! After three of these, shift to inhaling through the left nostril and exhaling through the right (not through the mouth). This time feel the opening of your centers. As you do this left-right nostril breathing, keep your focus on the third eye and crown chakra, letting the other centers open toward these two. This will not be difficult because the sixth and seventh centers have a natural *magnetism*—just as the snake charmer's music.

When you have finished this breathing pattern, go through the prayer again slowly, directing your attention to each chakra as you recite the phrase and key word.

RISING AND BATHING BREATH

Then, begin the second breathing pattern. It goes like this. Breathe through your nostrils in a normal manner; however, with each *inhalation* feel or imagine the life force being drawn up from the lower parts of the torso to the crown of the head and over into the third-eye center. Hold the breath slightly, and then as you *exhale*, feel or imagine the life force bathing the chakras as it descends through them to the lowest center. Pause, then inhale while again feeling or imagining the drawing upward. Repeat this cycle at a comfortable pace—using your consciousness and breath to direct the movement in synchronization with the inhalations and exhalations. As the breath and life force rise, feel or imagine how they are cleansed and purified in the higher chakras. As they descend, feel how they bathe the chakras with this purified energy. Take your time; again, consider this as part of the meditation. Do about seven cycles of inhalations and exhalations.

THE RISING INCANTATION

After this breathing pattern is a good time to use a rising incantation. Here's one from an ancient Egyptian mystical practice described in the readings. Breathe in

deeply, then as you very slowly exhale, direct your consciousness to the lowest chakra and begin moving the
life force upward as you chant in a drone "ah ah ah ah
ah, a a a a a, e e e e e, i i i i i, o o o o o, u u u u u, m m m m
m." Each sound is associated with a chakra. "Ah" with the
root chakra (reading 2072-10, "this is not R, but Ah," as
the "a" in *spa*). "A" with the lyden center (sounds like long
"a" in *able*). "E" with the solar plexus (sounds like long
"e" in *eve*). "I" with the heart (a long "i", as in *high*). "O"
with the throat (long "o" as in *open*). "U" with the pineal
(sounds like the "u" in *true*) . And, "m" with the third eye
(like humming the "m" in *room*).

Remember that true incanting is an *inner sounding*
which vibrates, stimulates, and lifts the life force. It is
done in a droning manner, with a monotonous, humming tone—vibrating the vocal cords and then directing
this vibration to the chakras, thus vibrating *them*. Feel
the chakras being tuned to the specific sound/vibration,
and then carry your consciousness upward as the sound
changes. Do this chanting three or more times, or until
you feel its effect. You may also want to finish this chanting portion of the practice with a few soundings of the
great OM chant (as in *home*).

THE HELD BREATH

Now let's move on to the next breathing pattern. It is
the more powerful, but by now you will be in a higher
state of mind and heart, and therefore, ready to further
release the life force and open the chakras. Remember,
however, that this is a good time to draw on the power
and protection of the Christ. Let your love of God-Consciousness and the image of the Anointed One within
you cleanse you and enable you to pass through it to the
Infinite. Now, with the Anointed One's protection and
power, begin the next breathing pattern.

This pattern is the same as the previous one except

that you will be *holding* breath until it cannot be held any longer. When the body begins to resist holding the breath, use all the alertness and "screaming" of your bodily cells to call forth the life force to the higher centers. The body may shake slightly (as Cayce's did occasionally), the temperature may rise slightly, but so will the life force, followed by the soul. Hold the breath with the consciousness focused at the crown chakra and third eye. Then exhale as slowly as you can, yet, empty the lungs. Rest here; let the body settle down. Breathe normally for a few cycles. Then, inhale deeply again, feeling the rising of the life force toward the higher chakras. Hold the breath at the crown and third eye. Keep the purpose clear and present throughout the body—"Raise the life force of my being in the love of God-Consciousness." This is a very good mantra or statement-of-purpose to use throughout this breathing pattern. It embodies the first commandment, *Love God with all your being*. The body will become concerned and excited about the breath being held. It must be guided by the mantra to understand why this is being done. Remember, the readings have taught us that every cell in the body has consciousness, and that consciousness can be raised or lowered. We are now using one of the more powerful methods for raising it. Do about three cycles of this held-breath pattern.

Important Note: Do not go so far beyond your physical, emotional ability that you break! Develop step by step, slowly yet with effort. It's like becoming a long-distance runner. You don't go out on your first day and run five miles. If you do, you will not be able to run at all tomorrow. You build up to it, running a little more each day as your body and understanding grow and adjust. So it is with these powerful breathing exercises. Build up your strength and understanding. Eventually, you will be stronger and more capable of taking the body, mind, and soul to places beyond normal physical life, just like a marathon runner. Push yourself to grow and develop, but don't break. You alone know when you are pushing too much. Success with any training that takes you beyond your present abilities automatically requires that you stretch beyond your present abilities, but do it in increments that allow your system to make the necessary adjustments for the new abilities to manifest. Otherwise, you will do more harm than good. Make haste, yes—but slowly!

> These exercises [yoga breathing] are excellent . . . Thus an entity puts itself, through such an activity [yoga breathing], into association or in conjunction with all it has EVER been or may be. For it loosens the physical consciousness to the universal consciousness . . . Thus ye may constructively use that ability of spiritual attunement, which is the birthright of each soul; ye may use it as a helpful influence in thy experiences in the earth."[13]

Often at this point in the meditation, the head will be drawn back, the forehead and crown may have pronounced sensations or vibrations, and the upper body and head may be moving back and forth, or side to side, or in a circular motion (circular is preferable). These are all natural results of the practice and are identified as such in the readings.[14] In the Revelation, St. John associates body-shaking ("earthquakes") with the opening of the sixth chakra, followed by "silence in heaven" as the seventh chakra opens.[15]

In to the Mind

Now we want to move in consciousness, so let the breathing and body go on autopilot (the Autonomic Nervous System will watch over them).

At this point in the practice, the whole of the body, mind, and soul are aroused and alert. Now, *the ideal held is the* formative *influence*, and development proceeds according to the ideal held.

The mind has a somewhat different experience in this type of meditation than it does in the Magic Silence method. All self-initiated activity is suspended. The mind has been changing as we have raised the energies of the body. By now it is very still, yet, quite alert. Stay here. Do not draw away or attempt to affect anything. Heightened expectancy and alertness is an excellent state of mind at this point. Here's where we have the greatest opportunity to *receive* God. Completely open your consciousness to God's. St. John says that he was "in the spirit" (the readings says this was John's way of saying that he was in meditation) and he "turned" (in consciousness) and his revelation began. St. John's word "turned" so precisely describes the cessation of all self-initiated activity. We too must reach a point in the meditation where we turn around from our constant outer-directed thoughtstream, to become transfixed on God's consciousness, and purely receptive.

Expansion and the Imaginative Forces

The readings say we should have a strong sense of expansion and universalization while in this state. They also recommend that we *imagine* expansion as we progress toward this place in the meditation.[16] The imaginative forces should be used to help us reach higher consciousness. So, imagine *expansion* as you raise the life force in the early stages of the practice. According to the readings, the pineal's primary functioning is "the impulse or imaginative" force.[17] It is the pineal chakra that aids in the transition from heightened material consciousness to real spiritual consciousness. Use your imaginative forces to aid in this transition. Also, reading 294-141 adds, "Keep the pineal gland operating and you won't grow old—you will always be young!" Again we see the rejuvenative powers of stimulating the imagination.

The Lower and Upper Gates

Reading 281-13 describes more of what occurs. "The spirit and the soul is within its encasement, or its temple within the body of the individual—see? With the arousing . . . it rises along that which is known as the Appian Way, or the pineal center, to the base of the brain, that it may be disseminated to those centers that give activity to the whole of the mental and physical being. It rises then to the hidden eye in the center of the brain system, or is felt in the forefront of the head, or in the place just above the real face - or bridge of nose, see?"

The soul is encased in the second chakra of the body, the lyden center. From this chakra it is drawn upwards by the magnetism that results from stimulating the pineal center. It rises to the base of the brain and into the pineal center, the crown chakra.[18] In ancient Egyptian mysticism, the lyden center is represented by the lower gate and pharaoh of the lower Nile, while the pineal center is the upper gate and pharaoh of the upper Nile. In *The Book of the Master of the Hidden Places*, there are ancient Egyptian pictures of a young man named "Ani" encouraging his soul to pass through the lower gate, and later Ani's soul is seen at the threshold of the upper gate, ready to make that wonderful passage into the higher consciousness. The caption under these pictures reads, "Hail ye gods who make souls to enter into their spiritual bodies. Grant ye that the soul of the reunited Ani, triumphant, may come forth before the gods, and that his soul may have peace in the Hidden Place."

A More Wonderful Life

The power gained from this type of meditation is not used to rule but to allow more of *God's* influence to come into our lives and into this dimension. Raising the Life Force within the body is key to higher consciousness and resurrecting mortal flesh as spiritualized flesh.

We are the channels of God in this realm, if we choose to be so. We could literally transform this realm if more of us developed ourselves to be better, clearer channels of the Life Force, the Great Spirit, God. The residual effect of this is that our individual lives become more fulfilled, abundant, rejuvenated, and eternal.

Success is in the *Doing!*

From the readings' perspective, "In the doing comes the understanding"—not in the talking, the reading, the believing, the knowing, or thinking—but in the *doing*. So come, take up your practice. Not just to feel better, but that the infinite may manifest in the finite, lifting all to a more wonderful life!

Why Meditate?

"I just can't find time for it."
"I just don't see the value in it."
"I'm not very good at it."

Why meditate? When we feel moody, out-of-sorts, overworked, tired, frustrated, why meditate? When we find ourselves whiny, or angry, or depressed, or weary, or any of the many feelings that human life brings, why meditate? When we can't quiet our minds because there are so many pressures, so many things that need attention, why meditate? When we are bored, why meditate? When we are sick or our loved one is sick, why meditate?

The answer to this question, "Why meditate?", is both simple and complex, requiring some willpower and faith. The answer goes like this: As individuals we have only a limited amount of energy, strength, wisdom, and power to affect change in our lives. As the Master asked, "Who among us, by taking thought, can change one hair on their head, or add an inch to their stature?" In the normal, human, *individual* condition, the answer is "None of us." But there is another condition that we CAN get into. In the *universal* condition, with the spiritual influences flowing, any one of us can effect change in our lives and the lives of those around us. This is the real reason for finding time and space to meditate. As a human individual we can do little, but as the universal forces find more presence within our minds and bodies, we become potent beings of the Life Force.

> As the body-physical is purified, as the mental body is made wholly at-one with purification or purity, with the life and light within itself, healing comes, strength comes, power comes.
>
> So may an individual affect a healing, through

meditation, through attuning not just a side of the mind nor a portion of the body but the WHOLE, to that at-oneness with the spiritual forces within, the gift of the life-force within EACH body.[19]

"The gift of the life-force within each body"—what a wonderful statement. Within each of us is a latent gift waiting to be claimed. It is claimed by purification of body, and the mind being wholly at-one with purity. This correlates to the passage-in-consciousness stage in which the "earthly portions" are removed from the body and suspended above it, thereby leaving the body clear, clean, pure, so the soul can rise and the spiritual influences can penetrate the whole of our being. Then comes healing, strength and power.

> The nearer the body of an individual draws to that attunement, or consciousness, as was in the Christ Consciousness, the nearer does the body become a channel for LIFE—LIVING life—to others to whom the thought is directed. Hence at such periods, these are the manifestions of the life, or the spirit, acting THROUGH the body.
> Let these remain as sacred experiences, gathering more and more of same—but remember, as such is given out, so does it come.[20]

I particularly like the explanation that many of our deep meditation experiences are the manifestions of the life or spirit acting *through* our bodies. After all, our bodies are atomic structures:

> The body-physical is an atomic structure. Each atom, each corpuscle, has within it the

whole form of the universe—within its OWN structure. Each individual body must bring its own creative force in balance about each of the atomic centers in order for the resuscitating, revivifying to occur in the body.

The law then is compliance with the universal spiritual influence that awakens any atomic center.[21]

It is simply a matter of natural and divine law: If we remain in the individual, human condition, then we have limited potency in dealing with life's challenges. However, if we open ourselves regularly to the "universal spiritual influence," then human conditions are tempered by these forces, and these forces are life and light, with power to make all things new.

What moves the spirit of life's activities? GOD, but Will and Choice misdirect. [22]

Meditation helps our will and choice be in accord with God's. Then life's activities move *with* the Divine Influence.

When is the best time to meditate? Here's a great answer from Cayce: "The best hour for meditation is 2:00 o'clock in the morning. The better [is] that set as the period in which the body and mind may be dedicated to it. Then keep thy promise to thy inner self, and to your Maker, or that to which ye dedicate thy body, mind, and soul."[23]

3

PASSAGE IN CONSCIOUSNESS

*N*ot so long ago, a very special spring struggled to break the hold of an unusually hard winter as I was try-ing to break out of a long period of personal struggle, a hard winter of my own. Reflecting on my difficult situa-tion, I recalled the perplexing comment in the Edgar Cayce discourses: "Though the tears may flow from the breakup of the carnal forces within self, the spirit is made glad . . . "[1] Well, I was happy for my spirit, but I was weary of the battle with the carnal forces, as he called them, and ready for some of that gladness to manifest in my life. Another Cayce discourse said, "For those things that are cares of the flesh and of the earth *cannot inherit eter-nal life.* Hence, life *alters,* life *changes* . . . and thus ye learn thy lessons, even as He; for though He were the Son, though ye are His sons and daughters, yet must ye learn obedience through the things that *ye* suffer. For ye have partaken of sin . . . as Adam, therefore ye must, as the new Adam, learn that God *is* merciful, is love, is justice, is patience, is long-suffering . . . "[2] [my italics] Well, at this point in my life, I was ready for the mercy. Then, to my great joy, through a combination of my own actions and a fortunate turn of events, I found myself free of the struggles and with plenty of one of the most valuable commodities of modern life, free time! All I wanted to do with the free time was re-study the Cayce volumes, meditate, and receive guidance through my dreams.

I began with the discourses that Cayce gave for himself—the 294 series—and went on to the 254 series, known as the "work readings," which included many that focused on Cayce's psychic process. I subsequently studied the 900, 137 and 3744 series. I wasn't looking for anything in particular, I just wanted that uplifting feeling I always get when reading the Cayce discourses. They connect me with something greater than my material life, while at the same time giving my material life purpose and meaning. This time I got more than an uplifting feeling. As I read, I began to notice a very peculiar practice described in sometimes vague but increasing detail. These discourses seemed to be guiding select individuals toward a practice that would help them make *passage through levels of consciousness.* Although I had studied the Cayce material for over twenty-five years, I had never noticed these instructions before, perhaps because the method is described in bits and pieces scattered through different discourses. Whatever the reason, I was surprised and pleased to have discovered something new, and I had all the patience needed for the task of gathering and collating Cayce's many comments, descriptions, instructions, and intimations concerning the practice.

The practice was similar to meditation yet at the same time quite different. The 294 and 254 series of discourses helped the outer man, Edgar Cayce, to better understand the mechanics of his great ability. They described the realms he made passage through and how his passage occurred. They explained why he couldn't always give a reading, or had difficulty in giving one, or why something strange happened during a reading[3]—all adding to my greater understanding of the nature of the process. I was even beginning to draw a *map of consciousness*, adding to it every time I found another detail.

In addition, I studied the discourses for brothers Morton (900) and Edwin (137) Blumenthal, the New York stockbrokers who were generous patrons of the work during the 1920s. Edwin's readings instructed him how to do what Cayce did, for he was told he would be able to do a better job than Cayce:

> Q. Will Edwin Blumenthal be able to give psychic readings like Edgar Cayce?
>
> A. The development is *beyond* those conditions as given by Edgar Cayce, for they will become conscious conditions to be acted upon by the conscious mind . . . [4] [my italics]

Morton, the elder brother, had a keen mind. Some of the answers to his penetrating questions gave me valuable insights into the nature of consciousness and the process of making passage through these realms.

The 3744 series was given for a group seeking to further understand the nature of consciousness and psychic ability. This series gives details about how the inner realms are arranged and how to make passage through them. Morton would often build his questions upon the answers given to the 3744 group, which helped clarify many ambiguities.

At this point you may be thinking that this was a method for giving psychic readings, but it was much more than that. By reviewing all of these discourses as a body of work, I detected that the "sleeping" Cayce was giving seekers *a map* of the inner levels of consciousness with *instructions* for making conscious, semi-conscious or unconscious (as Cayce did) passage through these realms—for greater *spiritual* understanding and discernment. Here's one example:

> The source may be from the subconscious forces of the body itself, or from the realm of spirit force as may surround the body, or a combination of both, or from a universal consciousness that is the source of life itself . . . Be satisfied with nothing short of *a universal consciousness*, guided or guarded by the Lord of the Way, or the WAY itself. In Him is Life! Why be satisfied with a lesser portion than a whole measure?"[5]

In other words, we could achieve several different levels of attunement from which our perspective would be realized, but the best level was the highest spiritual level from which we gain the better perspective. I set it in my mind to seek to attune to Universal Consciousness, protected and guided by the forces I perceived to be the highest.

Then, perhaps explaining why the Cayce discourses are considered the best in the world, we have this insight, " . . . in this body lying here, Edgar Cayce, we find all life in suspension, only portions of the higher vibrations in accord with those vibrations that communicate with the *Universal* forces."[6] This ability to suspend all individual life-force and make the higher vibrations in accord, or in attunement, allowed Cayce to communicate with the

Universal forces. That is ultimately what Cayce hoped for with each student of this practice.

His guidance often equated *psychic* with the soul, so psychic information was information from and about the soul and the soul realm. For example, "The psychic forces are the projection of the soul development in the earth plane."[7]

Yet, these instructions encourage passage *beyond* soul realms into the spiritual realms, equating spirit with God.[8] This fits well with Jesus' teaching to the woman at the well: "God is spirit, and seeks same to worship Him."[9] Readings 281-16 and -31 also correlate this practice with St. John's revelation, saying that John was in deep meditation when he made a breakthrough from normal consciousness to being, as John put it "in the spirit," and thus began his revelation.

As might be expected, I began practicing this method regularly in hopes of making a spiritual breakthrough of my own. I hungered for it, and was oh! so ready. At first, I found the method difficult. I couldn't discern the "landmarks" of his map of consciousness. I couldn't seem to make the transition he wanted from outer consciousness to deep inner consciousness (and yet, I had been faithfully meditating for more than twenty-five years). Though this practice was different than standard meditation, I knew that my many years of meditating were an asset to me now.

The first stage of the practice is to "subjugate" the personality and earthly portion of our being to the control of one's soul and subconscious mind.[10] Subjugation literally means, "to put under a yoke." I find it very interesting that the ancient Sanskrit word for yoke is "yoga." Could Cayce be selecting this word purposefully? If so, then we are to learn the yoga of setting aside our outer nature and putting it under the control of our inner nature, and finally attuning our inner nature to the Universal. Here are several quotes on subjugation:

> [When] the physical is subjugated or laid aside, we find the soul forces give the information, and the body is under the subjugation of the soul and spirit forces."[11]

> . . . the physical condition is subjugated to the psychical or spirit and mental forces of the body, and these produce the abnormal conditions . . . "[12]

> That lying between the soul and spirit forces within the entity . . . is reached more thoroughly when the conscious mind is under subjugation of the soul forces . . . "[13]

> When the physical body lies in slumber, we find the organs [of the body] . . . are subjugated, [and] the life-giving flow and the subconscious forces *acting*, and the soul forces ready for that communication . . . "[14]

> . . . through the universal consciousness or cosmic consciousness from the very abilities of the entity Edgar Cayce to wholly subjugate the physical consciousness as to allow the use of the physical organs that may be attuned to all realms that pertain to psychic or mental or spiritual influences in the realms about the entity."[15]

I had spent most of my life thinking of myself as the being found in my personality and conscious mind, so it was very difficult to set this so completely aside as to turn over control to some deeper being within or beyond my personality. It took me several weeks of practicing twice a day before I could sense this deeper me within me. It turned out to be extremely subtle, yet, clearly distinct. An early experience went like this:

I was slowly awakening from a night's sleep, dreaming, and very much aware that I was dreaming and exactly what I was dreaming. I was very comfortable, continuing to go through the dream in my mind. Then I got up and went to the bathroom. When I returned to my bedside to write the dream in my journal, I was surprised that I could not remember the dream. It was completely gone, as though I had never had it. As I lay down, I began to do the spiritual breakthrough practice in an effort to recapture the dream, as well as understand how I could have lost it so quickly and completely. When I got to a certain level in the practice, as though from out of nowhere, the realization came to me. This was a clear example of the distinction between the inner me, who had had the dream and with whom I was very comfortable, and the outer me, who did not have the dream but took control of consciousness when I moved the body to leave the room. I didn't remember the dream because the me that sat on the bed was not the me who had been dreaming. For the first time I realized just how thin, yet, opaque the veil of consciousness is. The shift in consciousness was so subtle that I didn't notice it. I wasn't able to discern when I was in one consciousness and not in the other. I also realized how familiar I was with my inner self, my soul. It was *me*. Of course, so was the outer me. Yet, they were separate and distinct—even the contents of "their" minds were different.[16] When I was in my dreaming self, I considered it to be *me*. I said *I* was dreaming. When I was in my outer, everyday self, I also considered it to be *me*. Yet, these parts of my being did not consciously know each other.

As I learned to discern the outer me from the inner

me (my personality from my individuality or soul) the practice began to take off. I began to see and feel what Cayce was teaching. Subjugation of the personality and conscious mind to the individuality (soul) and the subconscious mind was becoming a clearer, more identifiable shift or "turning," as St. John described it.[17]

In 3744-1 we are told, "With the submerging of the conscious to the subconscious, *the personality of the body and/or the earthly portions are removed and lie above the other body.*" On one occasion in New York City, Cayce was giving a "World Affairs" discourse for a group of people that were sitting in a circle around him. While the reading was going on, one of the participants wrote another question down and reached across Cayce's "sleeping" body to hand the question to the conductor, but he struck something above the body that no one in the room could see. When he hit this invisible something, Cayce's body went up in the air and landed upside down, even though the man had never touched the physical body. The discourse stopped, and they couldn't get Cayce back to consciousness. They rolled him back over and kept trying to give him the wake-up suggestion. It took them a very long time, and when he finally woke up, he yelled loudly, grabbing his side. They opened his shirt and were to surprised to find his side was black and blue, as though he had been hit. That afternoon, they got a reading to find out what had happened. When Cayce removes his personality and the earthly portions of his being, they are like a *thought-form*, somehow connected with his physical body. If one struck the thought-form, it affected the body.

The reading went on to explain that Cayce removed these aspects of himself from his body so that the body could become lighter, free of the earth, and that his soul, which abided deep within the body could move more freely. You have to understand that in the early periods on the earth (Lemuria and Atlantis), Cayce said we didn't even *use* personality. This is a development that came later. When you met an entity in the early periods on Earth, you were actually speaking directly to the soul, the whole of their being. Personality is of *this* dimension, Cayce says, and so he removes the personality and the earthly portions—very similar to meditation teachers who say, "Set aside all your earthly interests, all your earthly concerns; set them aside; get them out of the way." For Cayce it was like a *thought-form*; it was a real *form*; it had structure to it; it was really the earthly Edgar Cayce. So when the man *struck* the form, it would affect the physical body because the two are connected. When the thought-form came back in to the body, it brought the bruise back with it, and the body manifested that bruise.

As I continued to practice—to my great surprise—I too began to feel this removal and suspension of the personality and earthly portions of my being above my body. It was quite amazing to realize that personality is such a small portion of the total me. "When the subconscious controls, *the personality is removed* from the individual, and only other forces in the trinity [are] occupying the body and using . . . its elements to communicate, as in this body here [Edgar Cayce]."[18]

The Cayce readings imply that personality developed for two reasons. One was due to a shift from *spiritual conception* (as Isis conceived Horus when Osiris had no phallus) to *physical breeding* (as Eve did with Adam). Ultimately, Mary the mother of Jesus re-awakened to this ability and conceived Jesus by being "overshadowed by the spirit of God." Spirits can conceive using the spiritual forces. But humans breed by attracting another physical body to join with them. Therefore, humans want to project an appealing outer appearance.

The other cause was similar: when souls did not want

others to know their true feelings, they projected a partial truth. Projecting an aspect of oneself may seem innocent enough, and perhaps in the beginning it was, but when consciousness became too concentrated in the outer projection, consciousness of the whole being was lost. The deeper aspects of our being were submerged, and the personality became "unconscious" of them.

This concept changed my consciousness. I was breaking open to new vistas with almost every practice. Yet, I noticed in my everyday life that certain activities or people could quickly pull me back into my personality. I became more focused and experienced life from self only. When I was in my individuality (my soul self), my feelings and thoughts were more holistic. It seemed that I wasn't so self-centered, but more "group" or collectively sensitive.

I also began to experience some of the *physical* changes that accompanied Cayce's readiness to give a reading. Just as Gertrude Cayce watched for Edgar's breathing to become deep and his eyes to begin the "rapid eye movement" (REM) associated with entering the dream state, so I noticed that my "turning" from outer consciousness to inner consciousness was accompanied by *a shift in my breathing pattern* and *stimulation to my closed, carnal eyes*—as though they were seeing something while yet closed. When Cayce's breathing had shifted, his eyes were in REM, and his personality had been removed, Gertrude would give the suggestion to Edgar's subconscious to present the information being sought, and his soul would begin the passage to get the requested information. It was also at this same point that I would know that I had indeed subjugated my outer self to my inner self's control, and I would give myself the suggestion to begin the next stage.

The next stage is to *raise the subconscious to a higher level*, moving toward spirit or God-consciousness. As one moves closer to this level, one has to do with the individuality and subconscious mind what is done with the personality and conscious mind—subjugate them to the control of the spirit being and superconscious mind. Now here's where consciousness gets very uncertain. Edgar Cayce was "unconscious" of this transition. When he gave a discourse, his outer self would not be aware of any of the inner experience. Edwin Blumenthal was told that he "would be able to bring same to consciousness from the physical standpoint" and his conscious mind would be able to act upon the experience and guidance gained. Of course, he was told that this would not occur immediately—there would at first be "lapses" in consciousness, then semi-consciousness, but eventually total consciousness of the entire process. Edwin had a tendency to resist lapsing in consciousness, trying not to fall asleep. But discourse 137-5 told him "not [to] warn or fight against [these lapses] when entering the silence, and through such lapses will the first development show." They also instructed seekers not to "build barriers" that the subconscious would have to overcome, but "lend the assistance to the subconscious forces to direct."[19]

Morton thought the spirit and its companion, the superconscious mind, would descend into the earthly consciousness, but the readings said the opposite was required. One had to *ascend* into the superconsciousness, otherwise one would only experience the projections from these higher realms. Here are some highlights from this discussion:

> Q. What is this spirit entity in the body, Morton Blumenthal, and how may he develop it in the right direction?
> A. This is only the portion that develops other than in earth's plane. Spirit entity. For

soul's development is in the earth's plane—the spirit entity in the spirit plane.

Q. Does the spirit entity have a separate consciousness apart from the physical, and is it as the consciousness of Morton Blumenthal [900] when he dreams, or has visions, while asleep?

A. The spirit entity is a thing apart from any earthly connection in sleep . . . the earthly, or material consciousness is ever tempered with material conditions; [while] the superconsciousness, the consciousness between soul and spirit . . . partakes of the spiritual forces principally. In consciousness we find *only projections* of subconscious and superconscious, which conditions project themselves in dreams [and] visions, *unless [one] enters into the superconscious forces.*

Q. Does the spiritual entity, after leaving this earth's plane, have full realization of the physical life or experience through which it passed while on earth's plane?

A. It may, should it choose.[20] [my italics]

The readings explain that associated with this transition from soul to spirit, and from subconscious mind to superconscious, is an identifiable sensation of "expansion" and "universalization."[21] It wasn't long before I knew what the readings were talking about. I felt as though I had opened the door from the finite world to the infinite universe. My mind felt as though it rapidly expanded, containing a portion of everything that ever existed. I could see how Cayce could get information on just about anything and anyone. Physically, I noticed my head being drawn back and my body extending as though it too were expanding. The readings identified these sensations as indicators of progress.[22]

From this point on, one actually "leaves" the microcosm of "an entity," as the discourses call it, and enters into the Universal forces, or aspects of God's being. The first level is the Universal Mind and the Personal God. According to the discourses, this is also the level of the "Communion of Saints" or "Community of Seekers."[23] Often Cayce's spirit would ascend to this high level of consciousness to receive the "Book of Life" for someone seeking a reading. The "Keeper of the Records" would give him the book and often guide him as to what should or should not be read.[24] Occasionally, other souls or spirits would help with the discourse, or even contribute their own perspective or advice. These helpers included the Master Himself.

If you are familiar with Cayce's description of his own passage in consciousness, you know that in the lower levels of consciousness (lower realms of the soul) disincarnate souls were trying to distract him from his mission. At the middle levels (upper realms of the soul) Cayce would see others living life as though there had been no death. These souls neither distracted him nor helped him. Then Cayce would reach a higher level of consciousness (the spiritual realms) in which souls would help him with his mission. At this higher level, as I said, we come into the Communion of the Saints, the Community of Seekers, and the collective consciousness of all those who love God-consciousness and have attuned themselves to God.

As my practice developed and I began to become aware of reaching this Universal level, I too felt the interconnectedness of everything, or the "relativity of all force," as 3744-5 describes it. With the subtlest inquiry I felt I could receive a universal response. It is a wonderful place for a predominantly material person to be even *partially* conscious—just *being* there changed me. I came back nourished, comforted, at complete peace with myself, and my life. At the same time, I was fired up with the determination to fully realize this expansiveness in my *entire* consciousness, integrating all levels of my being into one wonderful, fully interconnected whole.

One of the most immediate results of this practice was a marked increase in my dreaming, dream recall, and the vitality of my dreams. It was as though my outer self had made a breakthrough into the world of my inner self, and now my inner self was going to make a breakthrough into my outer world as well. All the struggles of the previous years seemed to fall away from my consciousness, just as Jesus said when it compared the spiritual path to a woman delivering a child—"When she is delivered of the child, she no longer remembers the anguish, for joy that a child is born into the world."[25]

At this stage, I wanted to change my lifestyle completely, as did Edwin Blumenthal. He asked the question that I'm sure all of us wanted Cayce to answer: "Q. How can Edwin Blumenthal put his finances in such a condition as to permit him to concentrate to his greatest possibility on his psychic development?" Exactly the question I was asking at this time. Remember, psychic means "of the soul" in the Cayce work, so the phrase could have been " concentrate on his soul development," and this is what I was interested in doing. The answer given by Cayce was surprising and profound. It caused me to change my whole approach to soul development and spiritual breakthrough. It was: "Be not dismayed, for the development in psychic forces must manifest in and through the present conditions, and conditions physical, financial, must of necessity be one and a part of the development. As is given in this: In whatsoever state one finds oneself, make self content; not satisfied, but content, ever working toward that oneness of mind (of body, of will, with the development), or universal, or psychic forces. Do not war against these conditions. Make of conditions the stepping-stones to the development, necessary to meet the daily needs in physical, in mental, in financial."[26]

Once I accepted that my soul development was interconnected with the challenges in my life, and that using soul and spirit forces to "meet the daily needs" would lead to the full integration of my being and the Universal forces, my life changed dramatically.

The first dramatic example came through a dream. At the time, my wife Doris and I were financially struggling. We had about $500 on hand, but our obligations easily exceeded that amount. Here's the dream:

> I walk into a coffee store, where they sell coffee beans of all kinds. I tell the manager that I want to buy coffee at today's prices and sell it back to him later, when the prices go up. He says, 'You don't do that here. You do that at Merrill Lynch.' Well, I'm quite interested in this, so I ask him where Merrill Lynch is. He says it's 'just around the corner.' As I'm leaving, I notice a cashier ringing up sales on the cash register. I'm impressed with how much coffee they're selling."

When I awaken, Doris and I considered the dream and the promises in the Cayce readings that soul development and financial needs are to work together toward resolution. We decided to risk our $500 on this unusual dream. I looked up Merrill Lynch in the phone book and made an appointment with the commodities broker. When I arrived he asked me if I had a net worth of $100,000 or more. I told him I didn't have a net worth of more than $1,000 if he included both my cars and my first-born child! He explained that I could not invest in commodities, but I could buy an option on a commodity future, such as coffee. I asked him how much a future option would cost for coffee, and to my amazement, he answered, "About $500." Doris and I bought one option. Six weeks later he called me, "Your option is now worth $3,750. What do you want to do with it?" I answered without hesitation, "Sell!" Doris and I were excited. Soul development had proved to be quite practical and sensitive to our physical, financial needs, as well as our spiritual ones.

Two months later, in another dramatic dream, I was in a desert, looking at a mountain pass, knowing that something was 'coming to pass.' But I couldn't quite get the answer to what was going to come through that pass in the desert. As I began to look around the desert in search for an answer, I noticed a huge giant. To my amazement, he was standing on top of a flashing Exxon sign. Well, since I was watching for any dreams containing financial help, I called my broker again. At the price of options on Exxon, I could buy seven of them. A week after this dream Iraq invaded Kuwait, and oil went from $19 a barrel to $31. My options were suddenly selling for a much higher price.

I was impressed by the fact that somewhere within me was truly a Source aware of everything, even before it happened in the outer world—and that it cared to share that information with me for my financial aid; or, from another perspective, that I was allowed to come into consciousness of this for my personal gain. I want to point out, though, that these experiences seemed to be for the purpose of expanding my conception of what is possible, and responsibility for my financial well-being was then "returned" to me to work out in my everyday life.

I also had several dreams in which Edgar Cayce came

to me as an instructor, tutoring me in the development of this practice. Now, whether it was the actual soul-spirit known as Edgar Cayce or a symbolic teacher in the spirit of Edgar Cayce really didn't matter to me, although some nights I was sure it was the real Edgar Cayce. Here's one dream example:

It was a black, moonless night. I was standing in a boat in the middle of a vast sea. The water was black. The sky was black. The whole scene was dark and still. The blackness had the quality of secrecy, solitude, and quietness not evil. To my surprise, there was an island in the middle of this sea. As my boat touched the sandy shore of this island, I noticed a huge pyramid in the middle of the mysterious island. It was huge, reaching high into the black night. I walked up to it and began examining its sides. It was covered in ivy, but between the ivy and the stone was a layer of decaying fabric, much like ancient mummy wrapping cloth. It crumbled into powder when touched. I then noticed a ramp led up the side of the pyramid, all the way to the top. I walked the ramp nearly to the top when I "sensed" the sky changing near me. As I turned to look I realized that a door was opening in the sky. It was a door to a world or dimension beyond ours. Somehow I instantly knew Edgar Cayce was going to come through this door to talk with me. I knew he was coming from the world of the dead into my world. I became so frightened that I cried out to him, "Please, Edgar, don't appear to me completely; I'll jump straight awake and lose the dream! Please don't appear completely!" Edgar said "OK," explaining that he would simply talk to me from around the door's edge. I calmed down, leaned toward the door in the sky and listened. He told me things that were to come and what I was to do until *he returned.* Then he said in a firm voice, "Keep the light on until I returned." I turned and looked at the pyramid, there on the side of its outer wall were two light switches, just like those in our homes. I turned back to Edgar and said, "Edgar, you don't understand. Things are very difficult here. If I turn the light on, they will drive me out of here." He responded even more firmly, "John, keep the light on until I return!" I turned again toward the light switches and, mostly speaking to myself in a low voice, said "Okay" as I flipped the switches on. At the moment that I flipped them on, the dream went from dark blackness to brilliant lightness everywhere. I realized that the capstone of the pyramid was the source of this light and that it penetrated anywhere.

After the dream I synchronistically came across Edgar Cayce's discourse numbered 294-151, which predicts that he will indeed return in 1998! Not only does the discourse predict this, but it does so using an ancient Egyptian motif, just as my dream had! Well, this was nearly too much for me; my cup was truly running over. Life was expanding far beyond the daily mundaneness that I had been struggling with for so many years. It was wonderful.

In addition to my expanding dream life, I noticed a change in my capacity to love, and in the nature of my love. It was no longer personal or possessive. I seemed to have love for everyone equally, while yet knowing their weaknesses and meannesses. I would be around people

I normally did not like only to find myself more comfortable with them, more patient with them. This didn't blind me to their negative energy, but seemed to overshadow it with their *potential* positive energy.

My meditations have also improved. My body seems to be alive with the Spirit and a rising, expanding consciousness. I have clear sensations that my body is changing, that my spiritual centers or chakras are awakening and "rivers of living water"[27] are flowing through me. Now, that's not to say that life doesn't continue to have its mundaneness, trials, and disappointments, but they have become so overshadowed by the light of higher consciousness and the life force of the Spirit that I find, as Edwin was told, he too would discover, "the development gives ... contentment ... helpfulness, cheerfulness, loveliness—all of the perfect gifts as shown in a material world ... no matter what circumstances may arise ... "[28]

4

THE FUNDAMENTALS OF
PASSAGE-IN-CONSCIOUSNESS

A fundamental concept behind Spiritual Breakthrough is that we are *spiritual* beings manifesting temporarily in a physical dimension, and that the physical
body is a bio-spiritual instrument containing both the
physical and the spiritual elements of the whole being.
Therefore, the body can be used to integrate the whole
being. According to this teaching, the soul is manifesting in the physical body through the Autonomic Nervous
System, while the earthly self, the personality, is perceiving mostly through the Central Nervous System. By using these two nervous systems, one can make passage
from earthly, personal consciousness to spiritual, universal consciousness, as we shall see.

It is also a fundamental concept that the mind is temporarily divided into three parts: the conscious, subconscious and superconscious. These three parts may be thought of as three distinct planes of consciousness, or dimensions. The parts should be integrated, leading to full birthing of the true self. The true self is fragmented, living in the three distinct levels of conscious. In many cases, they are living a semi-conscious existence in these distinct levels. Birth, through integration, may be achieved by making passage through these levels of consciousness, then living a life that integrates the parts of the true self by allowing each to play a role on each level of existence. For example, on the physical level we must allow more of the soul and spirit to come through.

Within each of these three levels of consciousness are three parts: 1) a body, 2) a mind, and 3) a being. On our physical level we have the physical body, the conscious mind, and the personality. The "being" is the part of oneself that we call "me." On the soul level the "me" is the soul. Cayce called this the "individuality" to help us identify it as similar to personality, but different. On the spirit level, it is the portion of us that was created in the image of the creator, the godling or "god."

Here is the first of Cayce's *Maps of Consciousness*. This map is the territory within an individual "entity"—the term Cayce used to designate our whole being.

A MAP OF CONSCIOUSNESS		
The 3 Bodies	The 3 Minds	The 3 Beings
Spirit	Superconscious	"god"
Soul	Subconscious	Individuality
Physical	Conscious	Personality

Let's look at each of these levels in greater detail.

The Physical Level

The first level consists of parts we are very familiar with: 1) the earthly aspects of the physical body, 2) the conscious mind, and 3) the personality. These parts make up our normal, everyday selves in the physical realm.

It's important to note that the physical body, at this level, includes only the Central Nervous System (i.e. portions of the brain, the spinal cord, the nerves, the muscles, the skeleton, and the five senses). These are the functions of the physical body that are under the control of the conscious mind, and the desires and reactions of the personality.

Within the conscious mind develops the personality. As we have discovered, this portion of our being is influenced by heredity, environment, and socialization. The parents, the circumstances of life, and the physical dynamics of the body are powerful shapers of the personality. Nevertheless, as any parent can tell you, each child comes out of the womb with a disposition or attitude noticeably different from that of another child in the same family. This is the influence of the *individuality of the soul* manifesting in the body immediately out of the womb.

It's also important to note here that the personality, conscious mind, and physical body are new and developing. They have never incarnated before. This is their first manifestation and, broadly speaking, their last. It is the soul that existed before birth and will live beyond this life. That is why we don't normally have recall of pre-life existence. The memories are not those of the personality but belong to the individuality, the soul. The same is true of dreaming. The dream occurs in the subconscious; therefore, the personality does not have memories of the dream unless the experience is transferred to the conscious mind.

The Soul Level

The second level consists of parts that we are somewhat familiar with: 1) the inner aspects of the physical body and the soul body, 2) the subconsciousness mind, and 3) the "individuality." These parts make up our subtle selves, which are not normally seen during daily life but which play a dynamic role in our survival during the day and in our activity during sleep.

The inner aspects of the physical body are structured around our Autonomic Nervous System. This system consists of our organs, glands, sympathetic and parasympathetic nervous system, and all the systems that take over when the outer system is not or cannot take care of the body, such as during sleep or an accident that brings on shock or loss of consciousness. The autonomic system governs the temperature of the body, the heart rate, blood pressure, breathing, hormonal condition of the body, and more.

The Endocrine Glands directly correspond to the spiritual centers or chakras. These glands secrete hormonal messages directly into the blood stream. Because of this, these glands can affect the whole body. They can notify the body of any changes occurring (such as those happening during meditation, deep passage, and the like).

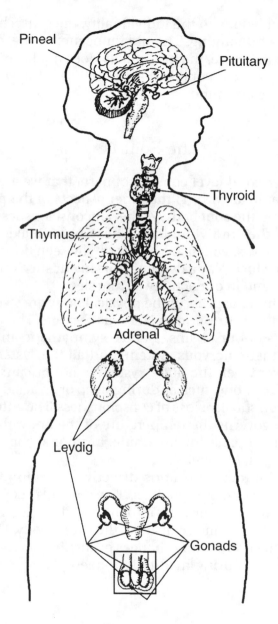

Diagram 1: The Endocrine Glands

The Endocrine Glands

These glands correspond to the chakras, or points in the body where the soul and spirit forces connect with the physical, and where the physical can contact the soul and spirit. Cayce does, however, slightly change the *order* that has been followed in recent centuries for the chakras, saying that the correct order was known during the times of the ancient mystery schools, but has been lost along the way. Here is his list and order:

Pituitary	Highest Center	Forehead (Third eye)
Pineal	6th Center	Crown of head
Thyroid	5th Center	Throat
Thymus	4th Center	Chest (Heart Center)
Adrenals	3rd Center	Solar Plexus
Leydig Cells	2nd Center	Just below the navel
Gonads	1st Center	Ovaries or testes

The rising energy follows the shape of a shepherd's staff or raised king cobra, running from the lower centers, up the spinal cord, into the base of the brain, over to the center of the brain, and then on to the forehead.

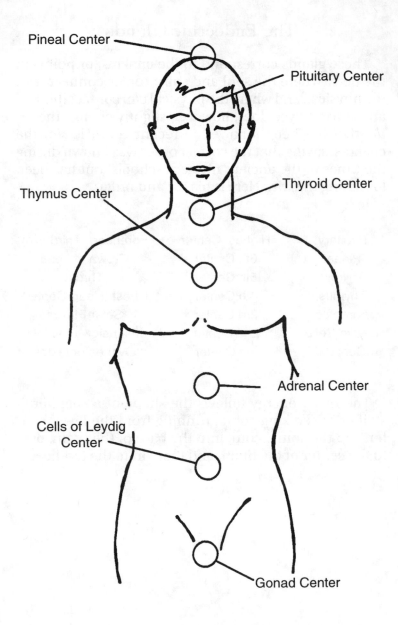

Pineal Center

Pituitary Center

Thymus Center

Thyroid Center

Adrenal Center

Cells of Leydig
Center

Gonad Center

Diagram 2: The Spiritual Centers of the Body

The Spiritual Centers of the Body

The Subconsciousness Mind is not an area that we are unfamiliar with, though it may seem so. Actually, we are quite naturally aware of this level but rarely make the distinction consciously. Remember my story in the last chapter, how I got up to go to the bathroom, quite aware that I was just dreaming, and suddenly realizing that I had absolutely no recall of what I was dreaming? This occurred because we dream in the subconscious mind (generally speaking), which is a very natural and familiar part of us, but we move and act in the physical world in our outer, physical consciousness, which is more disconnected from our inner selves than we realize. Thus, though we feel so sure *we* are dreaming, only an inner part of us is dreaming, while the outer part is suspended, not active, and not conscious. Then, as we move the body, which is only done by engaging the central nervous system and the muscular-skeletal system, we lose the connection with our inner selves and the dream is gone. We can't remember it because it is never a part of our outer self's consciousness. The key point here is that in the dream state, we are so comfortable and familiar with our inner, subconscious mind and individuality (soul) that we feel we are that mind, that soul. So, even though our outer self doesn't believe it has any knowledge of its soul, it does. Furthermore, this is an important reason for us not to think of Spiritual Breakthrough as supernatural, or that any of the realms or resulting powers are supernatural. They are only supernatural to our limited, outer selves. They are quite natural to our *inner* selves.

Another effect of this natural-yet-separated aspect of our structure is that we may often feel we have not had a deep experience during our practice when actually we have. The inner realms are so subtle to our gross, outer selves and so natural to our inner selves, that we may not realize we've been there or that we have had a significant experience. This is why we must develop some methods of transition to help us retain more of the inner experiences (whether they be dreams, visions, or meditative experiences). Before we do that, let's continue our study of the three levels of consciousness with the "being" part of the soul level.

The "being" part of the Soul Level is similar to our personality in the Physical Level. This is why the term individuality is a good one. The individuality is the unique complex of our being that is beyond the physical, survives death, and exists in the vast body of God as a unique point of consciousness and being. The soul reaches into the physical body through the autonomic nervous system, and into the mind via the subconscious. Just as the personality develops within the conscious mind and central nervous system, so the individuality develops within the subconscious mind and the autonomic nervous system. Unlike the personality, however, the individuality survives the death of the body.

The Spirit Level

The third level of consciousness consists of portions that we are much less familiar with: 1) the spirit body, 2) the superconscious mind, and 3) the little "g" god portion of our being.

The spirit body, as we have seen in the previous chapter, is "a thing apart from any earthly connection."[1] It does not normally manifest itself in the physical, material realm, except in projections. The Cayce readings use the conversion of Saul of Tarsus as an example of spirit/ superconscious projection into soul/subconscious and personality/conscious realms. Here's Cayce's comment:

"The spiritual insight was given into the heart and soul of Saul of Tarsus, as he beheld his Master in that realm to which [Jesus] had passed. The vision as beheld by [Paul], in the way that . . . the superconscious [of Jesus] manifests in [Paul's] subconsciousness."[2] Here's how the Bible records the experience:

As he [Saul] journeyed he approached Damascus, and suddenly a light from heaven [heaven being the superconscious realm of spirit] flashed about him. He fell to the ground and heard a voice saying to him, "Saul, Saul, why do you persecute me?" He replied, "Who are you, Lord?" "I am Jesus, whom you are persecuting; but rise and enter the city, and you will be told what you are to do." The men who were traveling with him stood speechless, hearing the voice but seeing no one [in their physical/conscious realm].[3]

Using the concepts from the readings, we could explain the event something like this: While riding a horse (or, in modern terms, driving a car), Saul's conscious mind loosened its control over consciousness (probably by the hypnotic rhythm of the horse's repetitive movements and sounds), allowing the subconscious mind to rise closer to the surface. As it did so, the superconscious mind of Jesus projected itself into Saul's awareness—and to some degree, the awareness of those traveling with Saul. Their physical senses of smell, taste, and touch were not affected, but they all heard the voice and apparently saw the light. Hearing is often the most sensitive perception. As the readings point out, during sleep most people's hearing stays on alert while all other senses are suspended.[4] Saul and his companions were able to hear the projection of Jesus' superconscious mind.

In order to really know or experience the superconscious mind and the spirit, we have to actually ascend to it or enter into it. According to the readings, this results in a feeling of expansion because the spirit realm and the superconscious mind are more universal in their awareness.

Now let's look at the highest part of our being, the little "g" god.

In the Cayce discourses, we have many examples and comments about this portion of our being. A good one presents itself as Cayce attempts to unravel the mystery of the Book of Revelation by St. John. According to these discourses, the disciples Peter and John traveled together much of the time.[5] When they were arrested, Peter was to be put to death, while John was exiled to the island of Patmos. As they parted, Peter said to John, "I will endeavor to keep thee in remembrance; even after my demise I will return to you."[6] Some time later, John was meditating on the isle of Patmos, "in communion with those saints who were in that position to see, to comprehend the greater needs of those that would carry on."[7] The angel that twiced appeared to John during his revelation was actually the "god" portion of Peter's being. It was his *spirit body* and *superconscious mind* helping John to see and record the vision. At times, Peter's godly presence was so beautiful and divine that John fell down to worship him, but Peter said, "You must not do that! I am a fellow servant with you and your brethren who hold the testimony of Jesus. Worship God."[8]

Each of us is a god within the Great God, and if we were to see one another's godly image we, like John, would fall down and begin to worship it as though it were God. As Jesus and the psalmist have said, "Ye are gods."[9] We have come so far from our direct contact with God, and put so many layers between us and God (e.g., priests, kings, churches, altars, etc.) that we have lost awareness of our godly place in the Collective God, Elohiym. In fact, this was one of the primary reasons that Jesus was condemned to death. He claimed that he was the Son of God. Well, no one was *that* close to God, so this was blasphemy, punishable by death. Nevertheless, the truth is, we *are* gods, have always been so, but we have lost awareness of this portion of our being and its place among the multitudes of heaven, among the Elohyim. This is the level of our consciousness that we need to ascend to or enter into. This is the spiritual breakthrough into Universal Consciousness, the Mind of God, where we will fully realize our true potential and purpose for being.

Here is another map. (See p. 86) This one is of the MACROCOSM (i.e., "the Universal") whereas the previous one is of our individual MICROCOSM (i.e., "the entity"). They both help us to see how we and the Universal dimension are structured. They also help us find our way.

View this map as a progression or ascent from the lower physical level into the many levels of the Soul (only three are given above), and then into the Spiritual Realm. When Cayce gave a reading, he perceived himself traveling through these realms. He described his journey something like this:

First, he would get into the stillness, the silence. He would look for or wait on the light that he always saw at the beginning of his passage. He felt himself as a speck or dot. Then, when he saw the light, he followed it intently. The first realm he went through was what he called "the borderland." It was filled with souls of a dark, self-seeking nature, some trying to distract him or grab him. He always managed to stay focused on following the light. He then saw souls ascending to higher planes beyond the earth and souls descending toward the earth plane. Then he came to a realm where souls seemed to be living life as though no death had occurred. There were towns and much activity. These souls didn't seem to notice him. Further on he came to souls who were

A MAP OF CONSCIOUSNESS

The Infinite One, Unmanifest

The Spiritual Level

God (Elohiym) / The Logos

Communion of the Saints / "gods"

Universal Consciousness / the Akashic Records

Souls who are "God-conscious" and
contribute to the Enlightenment

The Soul Level

Souls living life completely beyond the Physical
The "Borderland"—

Discarnate souls (some good, some not)

Incarnate souls sensitive to
more than form and personality

The Physical Level

Realm of incarnate souls, mostly experiencing
themselves through personality and physical form

Low levels of physical life:
"flesh pots," beastly, barely more than physical

very much aware of him and helped and encouraged him to continue on his journey, not wanting to distract him. Then, finally, he entered into a realm where the records of all the souls were kept. He would approach what to him appeared to be the "Hall of Records." The "Keeper" of the records would have the book or record of the particular soul for whom the reading was being sought. The Keeper would guide him as to what he could and could not reveal during the reading.

You can see how the map relates to Cayce's description of his journey from his physical realm into the Borderland (where many souls were of a dark nature), then on into realms where other souls lived. Later, he would pass into a realm where souls were quite advanced and took part in "the work" of enlightenment, and eventually, he would move into the realm of Universal Consciousness, where everything is known, accessible.

This description and map gives us a linear guide to making passage through the various realms of consciousness. But Cayce also gave another way. It was to perceive passage not a "going" somewhere, but as a change in condition. One is fundamentally the same throughout the process, simply changing the state of one's being—as water is always H_2O, yet, can be in different forms: solid, liquid, and vapor. As one goes into the silence, one changes from the "solid" condition of the physical-conscious life to the more watery soul-subconscious state, and then to the vaporous, cloud-like condition of the spiritual-superconscious. Using this model, we experience the passage more as a shift in our condition of state of consciousness. With the earlier, more linear models, we experience the passage as a movement from a lower to a higher state, expanding as we go. With both models, the ultimate goal is to integrate the three aspects of our being while becoming one with the Universal, the Infinite.

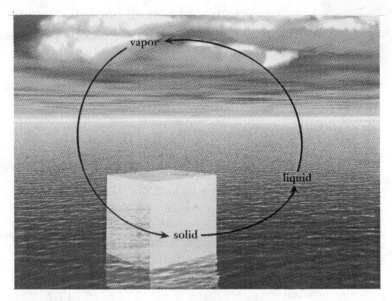

Artist: Jacob Dean

Diagram 3
A Change of Condition

A Change of Condition

As I used these maps and models for my own passage in consciousness, I did not see a light, but felt guided by the great power of my ideal combined with my imaginative forces. This seemed to move me through many distractions, on to the higher places. Occasionally, I would see a light, or feel what I perceived to be "the water of life," cleansing me as I passed through it or it poured over me. Sometimes I would perceive others. Most often, I came to perceive (or "feel") the many transitions associated with this passage, ending in a clear sense of universalization and expansion. Often it was very impersonal and powerful, far beyond anything like "me-ness." Often I felt like a very small portion of the massive Consciousness I moved into. At other times, it was personal, as though my own "Mother" had received me into her arms. I felt God so personally and directly that I understood what the readings meant when they said, "you will know as you are known." Despite my lack of knowing God, God knew me, and greeted me as a long lost child. I would come out of these practices filled with power and peace, and a sense that, ultimately, all would be one again.

In my case, being raised a Christian, I often search hard to know Jesus Christ's role in all of this. I found, like Cayce stated, that Jesus and Christ are two distinct qualities. Jesus is the powerful soul being who knew all of earth and flesh life, and sacrificed for me and others who believe in Him. Christ, however, is more like St. John's use of the word "Logos" in the first chapter of his gospel. This "Logos" or "Word" came and dwelt among us, manifesting through Jesus. I believe this is what Jesus was trying to explain to Phillip when he asked that Jesus reveal the Father to them. Jesus replied, "If you've known me, you've known the Father. The Father is in me." In my journeys into deeper consciousness, I found a central essence of all consciousness. This felt to me to be the Christ, the Logos that John was talking about. It was in me and beyond me. Everything had its existence in it. But I also came to know a portion that seemed to be different than the Christ/Logos. It was the unmanifested portion. A vast stillness that has no individualness or consciousness to it—it simply is infinite quiet, but a quiet that is teeming with the latent energy of life. I often felt the protective power of Jesus Christ as I moved through these realms. On occasions when I didn't, I found that I could find it if I'd only center myself and imagine it. Yes, I said imagine it. Imagining Christ's presence was one of the fastest ways I found to actually experience the presence of Christ when in the deeper mind. Imagination here is not fiction. It's creation! It's power! If you can conceive it, it is, much like Jesus' teaching about the power of faith and believing. Just a little of it can move a mountain. A little imaginative force in the realms of the mind can create. This is certainly why having a high ideal is so important. As Cayce often said, "You can create Frankenstein or a god using the same techniques. It all depends on the ideal held while using the technique."

Before we move into the practical side of the method, let me take a few moments to say what passage in consciousness is *not*.

Out of Body Experiences (OBEs)

Nothing of what I do is an OBE in the strictest sense of this term. In fact, Cayce had two people come to him who were doing OBE and he instructed them to change their practice. He said that OBE is simply disconnecting from the physical body and traveling around the third and, in some cases, the fourth dimension. What he wanted them to do was to go *within their own consciousness* to deeper dimensions of consciousness. This cannot be reached by traveling around the third and fourth dimensions in what amounts to the subtle body. It is truly a passage through dimensions of *consciousness*.

This follows Ouspensky's teaching that the dimensions are so perpendicular to one another that we cannot find the next one by searching through our current one. You may recall that Cayce recommended we read Ouspensky's book, *Tertium Organum*. In this book Ouspensky helps us to understand dimension travel by describing what it might be like for a one-dimensional person to discover the second dimension, and a two-dimensional person to find the third. If you visualize a cube being drawn, you'll see that the first line upon which a one-dimensional person's consciousness would travel is totally perpendicular to the second line to be drawn, or the second dimension. The next line is also perpendicular to the first two lines, as is the third dimension from the first two. (See Diagram 4.)

With this in mind, you can see how a seeker trying to expand his consciousness into higher realms would have to have an *altered* experience in order to find a place of consciousness that is perpendicular to anything he has experienced. Accepting this makes one more willing to surrender one's perspective, one's present consciousness, and reach beyond one's reality.

The key is to go WITHIN and then BEYOND the point of normal consciousness. As though one has gone through an hour glass, one comes out on the other side in dimensions much beyond this one—yet, they are surprisingly connected.

Lucid Dreaming

Lucid dreaming is an excellent example of consciousness in another dimension. However, I do not subscribe to the teaching that we should try to change our dreams from our earthly perspective of what is best. I never attempt to inject my outer self's will into a dream that I perceive is coming from my deeper self or the Universal Consciousness. I find this practice to be troubling. It doesn't fit with anything I've found in the Cayce readings or other spiritual teachings. I may be conscious, or lucid in a dream, but I don't attempt to affect the outcome of a dream using my personal will—unless it is clearly a part of the dream's intention and requirement that I make a choice or do something. In such cases, I

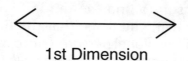

1st Dimension

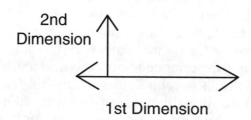

2nd
Dimension

1st Dimension

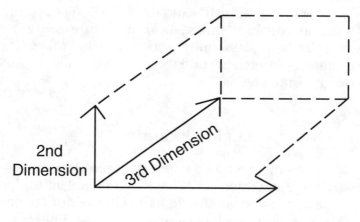

2nd
Dimension

3rd Dimension

1st
Dimension

Diagram 4
Dimensions

engage my will. Also, if the dream is more of a living experience than guidance from above, then I live it, using my will.

My own personal term for this type of dreaming is "living sleep." This term means more to me than lucid dreaming. It reflects my growing belief, and the readings' teaching, that we are often alive and active while in the worlds and realms of sleep. But that "we" is not our outer selves but our soul-selves.

On Giving Readings

I am often asked, in connection with Spiritual Breakthrough, whether I can give readings the way Cayce did, and whether I'd be interested in doing that. I have on occasion given readings as Cayce did. However, I do not feel that doing this is my life's purpose.

The readings say that some of us are more inclined to the psychic and some to the mystic. I am more mystical than psychic, even though I do receive guidance. I've met and worked with others who seem more "wired" for the psychic. I believe it may be related to soul-purpose, soul-experience. Some of us are wired more for soul perception and readings (the psychic), while others are more wired for spiritual insight and understanding (the mystic). Both are very important services, but require different "wiring." Of course, we all have both in us. One is readily with us while the other is latent, requiring development. Even Edgar Cayce, certainly a great psychic, had to develop his spiritual side, as we see in reading 5756-14:

> We find that more and more may the body
> Edgar Cayce grow to be more spiritual-minded,
> as it dwells upon those things that build for

> constructive forces in the experience of others;
> especially when and if the body is wholly
> cleansed from the carnal influences and forces
> in its material activity. Yet, the soul-conscious-
> ness may in any period soar to those realms
> where it has been active in all those forces and
> relationships in a spiritual or soul world.

Notice how the reading divides spiritual and soul, both as consciousness and as worlds. This indicates, again, that there is a difference between spirit and soul. The readings often equate spiritual with mystic and soul with psychic. Of course, they are ultimately one in the full understanding, but are separated for our develop-ment.

I have always been more inclined to the mystical ex-perience than to the psychic. However, lately, my mysti-cal practices have been yielding psychic development. I've had more precognitive dreams, more meditative and intuitive perceptions than ever before. From this I have come to assume that the two are tied closely together. If a person develops one to a high degree, then the other will also develop. When one person asked Cayce how to become more clairvoyant, the answer seems to be the practice of passage-in-consciousness itself:

> By the closing of self to the physical con-
> sciousness, and letting the universal con-
> sciousness flow through thy mind, thy body,
> thy soul; surrounding self with the awareness
> of His abiding presence with thee, ever.[10]

Let's move on now to the actual procedure we'll be using.

The Steps in Making
a Passage in Consciousness

TIME:

As far as possible, set aside the same time (and place if possible) every day for this practice, which can take as long as an hour. Such consistency helps the subconscious.

POSITION:

Lie down and put your hands over your solar plexus. If possible, lie on a north-south line. The head to the north was Cayce's direction for better physical alignment of the body; head to the south was for psychic/soul alignment. I suggest we begin with our heads in physical alignment (i.e. to the north) for the first few months. Then, after our bodies are in better alignment, we can turn around and lie with our heads to the south. Always cover your solar plexus when lying down (Cayce's instruction). When you are meditating sitting up, you do not have to cover the solar plexus. Passage in Consciousness is almost always done lying down.

> Optional Preparations:
> Fasting of thoughts, dedication of actions
> Prayer, devotional reading and/or inspiring
>   music
> Incense (frankincense, lavender, cedar)
> Stretching (head-and-neck exercise. etc.)
> Special covering (blanket, cloth, etc.)
> Incantation (om, a-rrr-eee-om, or vowels, etc.
> See Chapter 2 for instructions.)

(Specific suggestions for these preparations will be found in the chapters that follow. Here, we just want to list them for daily reference.)

Don't be intimidated by how complex this method may seem at first. In a couple of weeks, it will be almost second nature, and you may not even need to go through it in this step-by-step manner. It's a good idea to assimilate the basics, though. The list of steps will also help to slow you down, making the passage in a gradual and measured way, fully achieving a step before moving on to the next one. Transitions like these can take a long time in the beginning, so use the step "ladder" for now, and plan to discard it as soon as you no longer need it.

Preliminary: Lie down on a north-south line, placing your hands over the solar plexus. Do whatever you do to get relaxed, then begin. Follow these steps:

1. *Recall your purpose and ideal, say a prayer of protection, and surround yourself with a conscious sense of protection.*

2. *Shut out thoughts of the carnal life* (whatever this means to you). If you find yourself unable to do this at the start of a session, the readings suggest switching to prayer for a while, until you feel ready to attempt the passage again. We cannot make the passage with heavy carnal weight, even if that weight is in the form of thoughts. Shut these out. Lay them aside for the duration of the session.

3. *Put the outer self "under the yoke" of the inner self.* Subjugate the personality, conscious mind, and central nervous system to the control of the individuality (soul), subconscious mind, and autonomic nervous system. Conscious breathing helps to switch between the two nervous systems. Feel yourself turning over control of your body to your deeper, subconscious self.

4. *Remove the personality and earthly portions from the body, suspending them above the body.* Imagine this, feel this, and know that it is happening. Then maintain the suspension above the body throughout the practice period. (There's a much more in-depth look

at these steps coming up.)

5. *Feel the openness within the body.* Sense the lightness of your body as a cellular organism. Clear the thoughts, feelings, and attitudes you've added to it during this lifetime, including all of your current concerns. It's a wonderful feeling—light, buoyant, open.

6. *Give the soul the suggestion to rise up from its normal place in the second chakra.* Feel it pass through each chakra until it reaches the forehead.

7. *Notice a shift in your breathing pattern.* It will feel deeper and fuller breathing, along with a deepening of consciousness, as you pass into the level of the soul and the subconscious mind. Wait here until you feel the shift is complete enough to move on.

8. *Give your soul the suggestion to rise into the Spirit and the Superconscious mind.* Feel it rise up from its

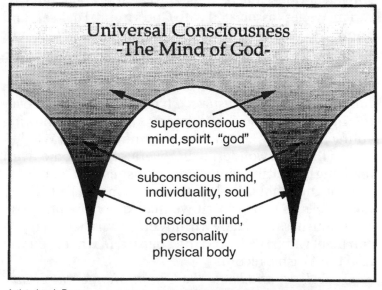

Universal Consciousness
-The Mind of God-

superconscious
mind, spirit, "god"

subconscious mind,
individuality, soul

conscious mind,
personality
physical body

Artist: Jacob Dean

Diagram 5
Human Nature: The Infinite and the Finite

normal place in the lower abdomen. Feel it pass through the body, expanding as it goes. Allow the time for this to happen at the soul's speed. *Inspire* the soul and subconscious mind to rise. Your ideal acts as a key to the door into the spiritual realm. Move into your spirit, your superconscious mind, your godly, eternal, and unlimited self. You will begin to feel a sense of *expansion*, and your breathing is likely to shift again—at first it may get excited as it senses the expanded, buoyant spiritual realm, but after abiding at this level the body will become so still that breathing will often become shallow. You will hardly need to breath.

9.   *Then, make the final movement into the Universal Consciousness of God, of which your spirit is a portion.* (See Diagram 5.) That is why there's no definite line between steps 8 and 9, between the superconscious and Universal Consciousness. Feel, see, and know the vast expansiveness associated with God's mind. Feel, see, and know the vastness, wholeness, eternalness of God's mind. (The remaining steps all take place within Universal Consciousness, the Mind of God.)

10.   *Human Nature, the Infinite and the Finite Abide in the Universal Consciousness.*   It is here you will discover the meaning, if you don't already know it, of "knowing yourself to be an individual, yet one with the Whole." One of the most wonderful discoveries in life comes with realizing that all individual consciousness is a "condensing" of the whole field of Consciousness. That's why Cayce tells us that "all that we may know of a universal consciousness is already within self."[11] It is here that you can meet with YHWH, and the Logos, and where you will find the Akashic records.

11.   *Feel, see, and know the Communion of the Saints,* those other souls/spirits who love God-consciousness.

12.   *Then, move beyond all manifestation and activity. Move into the infinite, ineffable One.*   Here is the

unmanifested Eternity, Life beyond action, thought or word—the Infinite Silence beyond and behind all life. You may experience this as the Mother, the Matrix, or the Void, and you are likely to feel great peace and great stillness. Surrender to this, the Source of Life. Rest here. Yield to It entirely. There is nothing for you to do here. Just be.

When you feel the session is drawing to a close, remember these three R's:

Retrace your steps so that you'll return fully grounded, with your normal consciousness intact. Descend back through the steps. This doesn't mean that you forget or let go of the feelings and experiences. You bring with you the essence of the experience, the higher vibrations and consciousness, but you integrate WITH your outer self and your outer life.

Rebalance the energies evenly throughout the body. Don't leave "supercharged" energy in the upper portions of your body, especially your head. Distribute it evenly throughout the body, including the inner organs of the body. This is *very* important. Even Edgar Cayce had trouble with this and was often reminded to rebalance the energies for normal operation in the physical realm.

Record what you have experienced. Write it down, or make drawings. This will help you anchor it in the physical world.

Intend to let the light of this session stay with you today, especially when you're with other people. Universal Consciousness can only come into the earth plane through our relationships. (More on this in Chapter 5.)

Now let's expand on those steps that will benefit from extra clarification.

Step 1: The Ideal, the Purpose, and the Prayer of Protection.

One of the best readings I've found for setting the stage for passage is:

> . . . first so FILL the mind with the ideal that it may vibrate throughout the whole of the MENTAL being! Then, close the desires of the fleshly self to conditions about same. MEDITATE upon "THY WILL WITH ME." Feel same. Fill ALL the centers of the body, from the lowest to the highest, with that ideal; opening the centers by surrounding self first with that consciousness, "NOT MY WILL BUT THINE, O LORD, BE DONE IN AND THROUGH ME." And then, have that desire, that purpose, not of attaining without HIS direction, but WITH His direction—who is the Maker, the Giver of life and light; as it is indeed in Him that we live and move and have our being.[12]

Again, Cayce guides us not to seek attunement in order for a certain, pre-conceived activity to be accomplished. Rather, seek to attune self in such a manner that God's Will and Way unite with us and imbue us with Its vision, wisdom and power. Then, we can discover our real potential—God in and with us.

When we practice, with all the excellent techniques that the readings have given us, let's remember the most important guideline: First, FILL self with God's will and guiding influence. Then, get the fleshly self out of the way and the magic begins—transformation in cooperation WITH God. This leads to the more perfect way.

The importance of a spiritual ideal is perhaps the most often repeated precept in the Cayce readings. The ideal held determines the outcome realized. Using the same techniques, one can make a Frankenstein or a god, depending on what ideal is held during the process. The ideal is the determinant. We use it as an image, a condition, a state of being that we hold as our ultimate desire—our *ideal* condition, image, or state of being. Here are some Cayce comments about the ideal:

> Ideas and ideals are quite different. One arises from the finite, the other from the infinite.[13]

> This is the nearest representation of that to which each soul seeks to attain: to be one with the universal consciousness and yet aware of itself. This ye alone can attain, in making the ideal that as was manifested by Him, who is the way.[14]

> Then the judgment, then the ideal, is that of the universal love, universal consciousness— that as was and is, and ever will be, manifest in Him, even the Christ—as was shown in the flesh in the MAN called Jesus![15]

> What IS ideal or what IS the ideal? In the term or sense indicated here, ideal means spiritual things, mental things, material things that are constructive in their nature, or that produce within the experience of the entity a greater awareness with the Universal Consciousness . . . [16]

A Prayer of Protection

Cayce advised that we never open ourselves to the "unseen forces" without first surrounding ourselves with a protecting influence. The following prayer was developed from several readings, some for the Prayer Healing Group (the 281 series), some for the Study Group (the 262 series), and some for individuals, such as 257. It is an adaptation of different versions found in these readings and others.

> *As we open our hearts and minds to the unseen forces that surround the Throne of Power, Might, Grace, and Mercy, we wrap about ourselves the protection found in the love for God-consciousness, in the thought of Christ-consciousness.*

For those not of the Christian faith, it is helpful to know that the Cayce readings occasionally replace the terms *Christ* and *Christ-consciousness* with *Messiah* and *God-consciousness*. Actually, the Hebrew word *Messiah* ("Mashiyach," Daniel 9:25) and the Greek word *Christos* both mean the same thing, *Anointed One*. We may call on this sanctified consciousness to protect us as we enter our deep meditations.

Finally, recall the number one purpose for making passage in consciousness: *To be conscious in the Mind of God, the Universal Consciousness*. Through this practice we seek to know ourselves, to be ourselves, and yet, consciously one with the Whole—the omnipotent, omnipresent One.

Step 2: Setting Aside the Carnal in Favor of the Spiritual

When our souls descended from heaven and first entered the earth, it was because of an attraction to the carnal or material forces. Not that these are to be despised in any way, for all life is one. But we must learn to be willing to set aside our attachment to the material and carnal for short periods if we are to find the spiritual influences we seek. Once we've learned to abide in Universal Consciousness, our relationship to the carnal and material forces will be transformed. We can then more actively serve as a conduit or channel for the influence of Universal Consciousness here in the earth. Notice Cayce's angle on this theme:

> Not that it, the entity, hasn't its own free will, but it—the entity or soul—develops either to a oneness *with* that Universal Consciousness or in opposition to same.[17]
>
> What is will? That which makes for the dividing line between the finite and the infinite, the divine and the wholly human, the carnal and the spiritual. For the will may be made one with Him, or for self alone.[18]

Steps 3 and 4: How Do We Subjugate Our Conscious Minds and Remove the Earthly Portions?

What do these steps feel like as I go through them? How long do these steps take? Here's my own experience.

In every case that I studied in the readings, the practitioner was advised to lie down, as Cayce himself did. While lying down, one uses the imaginative forces and the power of suggestion to move beyond the normal control and function of consciousness. Cayce used the phrase "see, feel, and know" to guide our imagination, and it works very well.

First, I see, feel, and know I'm moving away from my outer life and condition of being (i.e., conscious mind, personality, and central nervous system). How do I see, feel, and know? When I first began practicing I would use the "imaginative forces." These forces will ultimately cause the physical forces to move in the direction the imagination has been leading! So, in my mind's eye I SEE, in my body I FEEL, and in my heart I KNOW, or as Jesus instructed, I BELIEVE (in the deepest sense of that word).

Because the subconscious mind is always amenable to suggestion, one need only give oneself a strong suggestion that this shift in consciousness be made, *and it begins*. As I do this, my outer self (i.e., personality and conscious mind) begins to yield its dominant position to my inner self (i.e., soul and subconscious mind).

Now, let me walk us through it, exactly as I experience it.

I lie down, cover my solar plexus, close my eyes and relax. In my mind (sometimes, even out loud) I say: "Subjugate my personality and conscious mind to the control of my soul and subconscious mind." I will say this over and over. As I do this, I "see, feel, and know" my Central Nervous System is yielding its place—no muscular-skeletal movement, no sensory perception, and no outer-world functions. I feel my deeper Autonomic Nervous System becoming more conscious and in control—breath, heart rate, temperature, organs, intestines, brain, endocrine glands, and the harmony and coordination among them all. Often I will become more acutely aware of my body-posture, even to the point of making an adjustment in it: straightening alignment, stretching taller, releasing impingements and constrictions. I do not restrict my body from making movements to a better position that will allow a longer period of comfortable stillness. In other words, I'll use certain actions and movements to achieve non-action and stillness.

At some point during this transition I begin to feel the change has occurred, and then I really try to draw my soul and subconscious to the "surface," into a greater position of consciousness and control. This does not feel like someone or something other than me. It feels like me, but the real or deeper or more profound ME.

As this progresses, I turn over control of the Central System to my subconscious, which is very capable of taking care of it. As the readings point out, whenever we are in shock, or fright, or doing something monotonous, our subconscious takes control of the Central Nervous System. It's those times when, because of injury or fright, we say something such as, "From that point on I don't remember a thing and I have no idea how I got through it." That's when the outer self "lost it" and the inner self took over. It also occurs during those lapses in consciousness that occur because of monotony, such as washing the dishes or driving the car. We simply cannot remember driving that stretch of road, and yet, we did drive it. During those times the conscious mind is suspended and the subconscious is driving, or washing dishes, or dealing with the outer world. The subconscious has control of the senses and the body, and it does just fine. So it is as we move deeper into the realms of consciousness that Cayce traveled, and we travel.

Then, after I see, feel, and know progress is occurring, I imagine the removal of my personality and earthly portions from my flesh body. I visualize it. I feel it. I imagine it. And, it removes itself!

> When the subconscious controls, the personality is removed from the individual, and only other forces in the trinity occupy the body

> . . . With the submerging of the conscious to the subconscious, the personality of the body and/or the earthly portions are removed and lie above the . . . body.[19]

This earthly portion feels like a collective thought-form or an energy field, an energy field that is associated with my incarnation in the earth—an energy field that I have developed as I have grown from a baby to a fully incarnated adult. By the word "field" I mean a space within which "magnetic" and "electrical" lines of memory and sensation are active. The field has shape and space and personal qualities to it. The field is composed of my sensations (i.e., my fleshly experiences which have shaped my personality and earthly portions) and my thoughts and memories (i.e., my conscious mind). I feel it as a subtle form of my flesh body—actually me, the me that I can sometimes watch go through life. It slowly leaves my flesh body through the front, and suspends just above my flesh body, about three to six inches away. This causes my flesh body to feel lighter or emptier, more open throughout the kundalini pathway or, as Cayce called it, "the Appian Way." Yet, it doesn't feel completely disconnected because it can so quickly and easily come back into the overall body, even without me aware of it. I have to work at keeping it suspended and out of the way.

As far as time goes, it has taken me from five to forty minutes to accomplish this. When I first began practicing, it took me a good thirty to forty minutes to subjugate control and remove the personality and earthly portions. In fact, much of my practice was devoted to simply achieving these early stages. After three years of practicing, it would generally take me only five to ten minutes. But time is very elastic during these practices. I've had times when I was sure I had been under for an hour or more, only to find that I had been "gone" for twenty to thirty minutes. At other times, I've been under for up to two hours, yet, it felt like thirty minutes.

Step 6

As I practiced this, I found that if I *"shut out thought pertaining to carnal life" and imagined my personality and earthly portions being removed from my body and suspended above it,* that it actually worked. I really sensed something like that happening. It caused me to feel very open inside my body, as though something had been moved out of the way. Then, with the slightest suggestion, I imagined, and often *felt,* my soul rise from out of the second chakra to the base of the brain and then over into the center of the brain and the third eye, causing me to go even deeper into this altered state of consciousness. I would feel myself expanding and moving into a place beyond my body's finite location—a place in consciousness, not in the third dimension.

A—"The personality and earthly portions are removed and lie above the body."

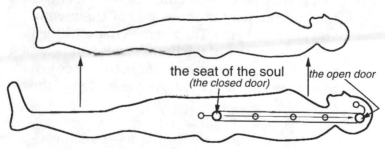

the seat of the soul
(the closed door)

the open door

Artist: Jacob Dean

B—The soul rises through the cleared passageway.

Diagram 6: The Personality and Earthly Portions Suspended, the Soul Can Rise Through the Centers

Here is a reading related to this process:

There are definite conditions that arise from within the inner person when an individual enters into true or deep meditation. A physical activity takes place, acting through the activity of the imaginative or the impulsive forces. The sources of impulse and imagination are aroused by the shutting out of thought pertaining to the carnal forces of the person. Then, changes naturally take place when there is the arousing of that stimuli within the individual that has within it the *seat of the soul's dwelling within the body*, then this partakes of the individuality [i.e., the soul] rather than the personality.[20] [my italics]

The soul is within its encasement, or its temple, within the body of the individual, see? With the arousing then of this image, it rises along that which is known as the Appian Way, or the pineal center, to the base of the brain, that it may be disseminated to those centers that give activity to the whole of the mental and physical being. Then, it rises to the hidden eye in the center of the brain system, or is felt in the forefront of the head, or in the place just above the real face, or above the bridge of the nose, see?[21]

If there has been set the mark—mark meaning here, the image that is raised by the individual in its imaginative and impulse force— such that it takes the form of the ideal the individual is holding as its standard to be raised to, then the individual (or the image) bears the mark of the Lamb, or the Christ, or the Holy One, or the Son, or any of the names we may have given to that which *enables* the individual to enter THROUGH IT into the very presence of that which is the Creative Force from within itself, see?[22]

Remember to use suggestion when you are ready to have the soul rise up through the centers. Movement isn't likely to take place otherwise.

The combination of "shutting out of thought pertaining to the carnal life," subjugating the conscious mind, imagining the removal of my personality and earthly portions, and the suggestion for my soul to rise—this combination had a profound effect on me.

At first, I'd come back to normal consciousness only knowing that something very deep was going on. But, as I practiced, I began to come back knowing that my body was changing, and that the condition of my existence or manifestation in this dimension was changing. Eventually, I found that I was quite conscious in the deeper places, and perceiving. Before this I was hardly aware of anything other than "strangeness," deep peace, and being in some sort of altered state. I once read where Cayce said that going over to the other side was very much like coming over to this side—It took some time to perceive the realm. As I reflected on my childhood and watched my own children awaken to this realm, I realized just how one must allow time for the transitions to be made and the perceptive forces to adjust.

Let's now look at the first recognizable transition as we move through consciousness in our practice.

Step 7

The transition from physical consciousness to soul consciousness is perhaps the most difficult transition to recognize, but Cayce gives us a fairly definite way to know whether we have reached this stage. I can attest to its effectiveness.

The key indicator that a transition from the physical/conscious level to soul/subconscious level has been made *is a change in the breathing pattern.* Usually this change is toward deeper breathing. It may also be accompanied by rapid eye movement (REM), imagery, and even sleep. These are all signs that we are entering the soul/subconscious level of our being.

The readings never criticized seekers who fell asleep during their practice session. He often said it was a natural result of the passage into the soul/subconscious realm and was the first stage of awakening; that eventually they would retain memory of what went on during the "sleep" period. They may eventually not feel that they "fell asleep," because some form of consciousness was maintained. Here's an example from the readings:

> The body should not attempt to consciously prevent the conscious losing itself in sleep or slumber, for through this we will find the first action of the psychic [soul forces] making the physical manifestation to the conscious mind . . . And, the conscious will find the developing of the psychic or latent forces in the present earth plane and may be able to use those manifestations for the development of self and of others. This is the correct way to develop the forces.
>
> Q. How will psychic [soul forces] manifest in the physical?
> A. First through the lapse of consciousness,

which the body should not warn or fight
against when entering the silence, and through
such lapses will the first development show.[23]

The progression goes from unconscious passage, followed by a period when you'll notice lapses, followed by
semiconscious passages. Eventually you'll be fully conscious. I'll give you an example. My wife, Doris, and I
were practicing together on the bed. We started the routine, and roughly an hour later, I finished the session and
found she was gone. I had been conscious through the
whole session; it had been a fantastic meditation. I was
surprised that I hadn't noticed her leaving. I walked out
into the living room and said, "Doris, why'd you leave
early?" She said, "How do you expect me to meditate
with you snoring as loud as a train going through the
bedroom?" "Doris," I said, "I never fell asleep! I was conscious the whole time!" She asked, "And you didn't hear
yourself snoring?" "Not at all," I answered. This was our
first indication of reaching the stage of being really unconscious of the body at the same time as being fully
conscious on another level.

It's a very subtle, but very definite transition, and it
takes time to reach it. Be patient, and believe that your
imagination and intent will get you there.

People who are working with spiritual breakthrough
sometimes ask me what to do when they feel stuck at a
certain place or when they have slipped back to a "lower"
level of consciousness. That's when I tell them about pla-
teaus:

Seekers enter into the silence and the deeper places,
reaching a level at which it appears that they can go no
further: a plateau. At this point, they may linger and even
cycle back to a lower or more outer level of consciousness before returning to the plateau. If they linger (or, in
Jesus' words, "Tarry in the upper room" of their con-

sciousness), a transition will occur, allowing them to break through to a higher or deeper level of consciousness. This cycle repeats itself until the seeker has reached

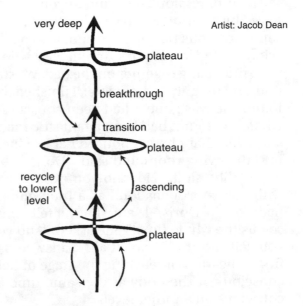

Diagram 7
The Typical Cycle of Deep Passage

very deep levels of consciousness. This is why the practice requires time, from forty minutes to an hour. It also requires patience and expectancy, or faith. As one tarries in Faith and Patience, many adjustments are taking place within the body and mind for passage to the next level of consciousness. This is how one gets into very deep levels of meditation, and eventually into the Universal Consciousness or Mind of God.

One last tip for this stage: We must be careful not to stay in the wondering, wandering subconsciousness mind level. It's a lullaby place of daydreams and loop-thinking about our problems and opportunities. We want to move on, inspiring our subconscious to rise upward into our superconscious and then on into the Universal Consciousness of God. We use our will to move through these specific stages.

Steps 8

Next, I inspire my soul to rise up and enter into the spirit and the superconscious mind. I simply say—

Arise my soul and enter into the spirit and
the superconscious, then on
into the Universal Consciousness!

The key indicator that a transition from the soul/subconscious level to the spirit/superconscious level has been made is *a sense of expansion.* Some people use the word *buoyancy* to describe this sensation. I simply feel that I've expanded. My conscious reach is beyond my senses and my body. I'm free of my body. Not like out-of-the-body experiences, more like my consciousness reaching far beyond body-confinement, even subtle body confinement.

This may also be accompanied by another shift in the breathing pattern, only this time the shift will be toward a more shallow breath, rather than the deep breathing pattern of the soul/subconscious level. However, I've often noticed that my breathing will briefly become excited when I sense contact with spirit and superconscious. Then, as I abide there, it calms to a level at which I hardly need any breath, just very shallow breathing.

Also, the body may begin to physically react to the spirit force's rising presence. However, this body response seems to occur in two different ways, depending on the individual or the conditions at the time of the practice. Some people, and at some times all of us, will feel enlivened, energized, and our bodies will shake or move with the influence of the spirit. Other people, and at some times all of us, will feel as though we "dropped of a cliff." It's as though we have let loose of the body completely. In this condition we will be impervious to physical stimuli, as Cayce was. When Cayce was in his deep state, you could stick him with a pin and he wouldn't react—until he regained consciousness, that is, and then he'd feel great pain.

So there are two ways we may react to the entry into the spirit/superconscious realm: 1) with great bodily stimulus, or 2) completely lose all sense of the body. However, the readings are pretty clear that as we enter this realm we will all feel a sense of expansion. They also say that we will notice our attitudes and perspectives being *universalized* because of our contact with the Universal Forces.

In the Universal Consciousness
Steps 9 and 10:

I visualize and feel myself (of course, I am now into my inner self) rising upward and expanding into the Universal Condition and completely out of the individual condition. This is a *wonderful* experience, very releasing and freeing. We have to remember that God is not a being like you and me. We are in a state of beingness or an *individual* condition. God is in a *universal* condition—infinite and eternal. For a predominantly finite, mortal person, this is a difficult transition to make—BUT IT CAN AND SHOULD BE DONE!

The spirit is the universal consciousness, or God; that which is the First Cause; that which is manifested in all the varied forms and manners that are experienced[24] . . . 826-11

Life itself is the consciousness, the awareness of that oneness of that Universal Consciousness in the earth.[25] 2828-2

The Universal Consciousness, the mind of God—to find this is to find our true Home. It is the Infinite Consciousness of which all individual consciousnesses are extensions. To say more than this would be an attempt to define and limit the Infinite. But you will certainly recognize it by its expansiveness and by how blessed you feel when you are there.

The readings suggest that we can work towards Universal Consciousness (which our spirits have never really left!), but we must live it or apply it in our relationships with others. If we don't, it will not become "real" to us.

When we return from this contact with God, the Infinite is in the finite, the Eternal in the mortal. That at-one-ment that is so vital to our salvation and resurrection comes a little closer to reality. Each practice session takes us a step closer to knowing ourselves to be our true selves, yet, one with God, the Universal, the Whole, that Infinite, Eternal Oneness. As the readings say, "Come to know that not only God is God, but self is a portion of that Oneness."[26] I am sure Cayce does not mean for us to know this intellectually, but to know it throughout our entire being. Know it by having experienced it firsthand, directly, repeatedly—fully imbuing ourselves with its transforming, reuniting spirit—gods within the Great God, once again! I want that with all my body, mind and soul!

We've probably already said enough for now about

these aspects of Universal Consciousness. You will want to do your own exploring and discovery.

Steps 11 & 12: There Are Two Aspects to the Godhead

One is the Universal Consciousness which includes the Communion of Saints, the Akashic Records, the Personal Father-God, and all Life in activity. The other is the vast Infinite One, unmoved, from out of which all else has found expression. This is the Ineffable One, the impersonal Whole. It is the "same yesterday, today and tomorrow." It is the womb of the Mother-God, totally nourishing, and the inner place of silence before the beginning. Allow yourself to experience and know all the dimensions of self and God.

RETRACE AND REBALANCE

The step-by-step method is powerful. It moves us into deep levels, levels that change the bio-electrical and chemical energies, and their concentrations, throughout the body and lower mind. Therefore, it is important to carefully retrace your steps back to this dimension and rebalance your system completely before trying to function in this outer dimension after a deep session. Take the time to retrace and rebalance. Make sure you do not leave supercharged energy in the upper portions of your body.

This does not mean that you shut off the higher vibes and consciousness that you experienced during the deep session. You bring these with you (at least the essence of these). But you must integrate them into your outer consciousness and normal vibrations. Balance. Balance. Balance. With balance you will be able to awaken your godly self while living in your physical self, and maintain some healthy sanity about it all.

KEEP RECORDS

In many mystery schools and in the Cayce readings, students/seekers are told to record their experiences and chart their progress. There are many reasons for this. One is that we have an amazing capacity to forget. Another is that we don't fully bring ethereal things into the physical realm unless we bring them out into our outer conscious world through words, written and spoken, and perhaps with drawings as well. Here's how Cayce encouraged it:

> In the study of such it would be well that . . . students chart the various physical phenomena as is their experience with sources, or source, of information . . . in that that may be termed an analytical chart. Not as seeking a formula, but that which takes place; and when studied, or when attunement is made by others, their *own* formula will be manifest. [Recording that which] lies within each entity, that awakens to the spirit of truth, or the essence of regeneration in the spirit of truth, that makes for the continuity, or the active forces in the spirit of life, or the essence of same itself. As has been given oft, no matter what phenomena may be manifest . . . there is some *form* that is assumed.[27]

We need to record the form our passage and development takes in order to fully "bring to physical consciousness"[28] the whole of our development.

I use a journal to record my impressions and experiences before, during, and after the practice of spiritual breakthrough. I also record, in another journal, my dreams, which have proved to be unfolding with profound vision and meaning for me and for those with whom I share life. The records have been an important source of support and confirmation to me through the years. True, there is no one formula, since we are all individuals, but my records have helped me understand my awakening and shown me how it relates to the awakening of others. They have also helped me not forget just how much I have received. Keep a journal. It will pay big dividends over the long haul.

TIPS ON CONTACTING GOD AND KNOWING IT!

In concluding this chapter, I'd like to pass on some of the lessons I've learned in my Spiritual Breakthrough practice. Some of these I learned when I felt really out of touch and was struggling to reconnect with God. I have found the following elements of thought, attitude, and action to be the most successful for contacting God.

1: Don't try to bring God down to us. The better way is to lift ourselves up into the Universal Consciousness.

This has proven to be the best way for me to contact God despite my pain or need or despair. This can be found in the readings, too:

> No one approaches the Throne or the Threshold of Universal Consciousness without the purpose of EITHER lifting self to that consciousness or bringing us DOWN to their own ideal.[29]

Notice how Cayce emphasizes the word "either." It's as though there are only two ways. It certainly appears that Cayce is encouraging us to lift ourselves up into the higher ideal and the higher consciousness.

When I'm down and struggling, this mindset can be very difficult to maintain. I have a tendency to whine and call for God to come help or guide me. Lately though,

I've stopped doing this, and simply forced myself to let go of all my "earthly portions" and concerns, seeking only to lift myself above the woes and into the higher states of consciousness. This leads us to the second mindset or governing influence.

2: Don't try to leap straight into God-consciousness.

For most of us, there are stages, transitions, and adjustments that simply must be made before one becomes conscious of God. These adjustments require some time and patience, no matter how anxious or needy we are. When I'm hurting, I allow more time for the practice, more practices, and a few days to get myself in touch. Sometimes it comes very quickly. Sometimes it takes a few days. Occasionally, it takes longer. If we try to go immediately into God-consciousness and if because of our earth-binding ache we don't succeed on the first try or within 10 minutes, we all tend to give up! Never trying again! Despairing that God has abandoned us. We need to seek, seek, seek, and the answer will come.

3: Stay impersonal.

Don't cry or whine. Seek according to the law, which is line-upon-line, step-by-step. Then, once we're into or near the Consciousness, a peaceful, unemotional, impersonal seeking seems to be the best condition for the expansion necessary to fully come into Universal Consciousness.

I find this to be one of the hardest aspects of this approach. It may be because we all want a personal God who feels our emotions, which I believe God does do, but in order to turn around and feel God requires that we become more like or attuned to God's nature. The Cayce readings and many other sources indicate that God's nature is not in the form of a person as we know him. God is not a person, though God can manifest in and through a person. In 1158-12 a seeker asked, "If God is impersonal force or energy—" and Cayce interrupted her right there, saying: "He IS impersonal." Cayce does go on to explain how God in His natural state, the state He says we will find Him when seeking within is impersonal, but as we let Him flow through in our outer state, He then becomes personal.

God is also more universal than we are, requiring us to move out of our individual condition and more into God's universal condition.

4: We must BELIEVE that God exists!
This must seem obvious but Cayce states it over and over as one of the key steps to full consciousness.

> So, as is seen in individuals that would say, "Yes, I believe - but." "But" meaning there is that doubt, [caused] in their experience when . . . that individual or others spoke yet acted in a manner as if that did not exist! Then, creating the doubt for self.[30]

> And he that would find the God in self must believe that He is, and proceed from that premise. He that believes that God is may approach Him within his OWN self.[31]

5: Don't look beyond ourselves for God.
This is difficult, but crucial. God is not separate from us. Therefore, we can be standing right in God's mids and not realize it because we are looking for God to objectify Himself. This reminds me of the reading for straining seeker who felt his requests were being ignored by the sleeping Cayce:

> Q. Why will you not answer these questions

when I want to make sure in order to help?

His challenging question draws the archangel Michael through Cayce:

> A. He that seeketh a sign when he standeth in the presence of the Highest authority in the Way may NOT be given a sign—unless, he has done in the body that which entitles him to same.[32]

It's obvious this guy did not realize that he was already standing "in the presence of the Highest authority in the Way!"

To overcome this sense of separation, I use the mantra, "God and I are one." I see, feel, and know this statement to be true. As I feel it coming upon me, I yield selfness, expanding into the Universal Oneness of God's being. Here I abide, imbuing myself with strength, peace, and guidance. Sometimes I actually begin to give myself, others, and the world, a reading—just as Cayce did. I ask questions of the Universal Mind and feel, see, know the answers as they come.

If you recall from Chapter 3, Morton Blumenthal was told to get to that consciousness where he knew that "not only God is God, but self is a portion of that oneness."[33] This is the mindset that helps me discern my proximity to God when I'm right in the midst of God. It's very subtle. There is no way any of us could be outside the Whole, yet we feel we are. In order to feel the Whole we have to suspend our sense of separated-selfness. Deep meditative session, such as passage-in-consciousness, help us suspend this feeling and re-experience infinite oneness and attunement to the Whole. As we do this more and more, we become consciousness familiar with the Omnipresent One, God.

5

Aids to a Deeper Experience

*O*nce you've started practicing passage-in-consciousness, there are things you can do to deepen your
experience other than the power of your own intention
and desire. Some, such as health practices, can be done
before "ascending the mount," while others, such as applying what is gained, take place after returning. By purifying the physical and the mental, we make the upward
path clearer; by applying what we've gained, we create a
more open channel from the universal consciousness
into the world.

These three focuses—universal consciousness, the
body-mind, and other people—form a triangle of relationships. We'll look at each side of the triangle in turn

(beginning with the left side), because all three pairs are vitally important to spiritual breakthrough.

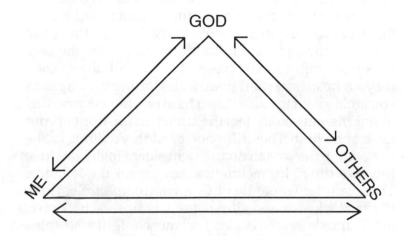

The Body-Mind and Universal Consciousness

One of the things we discover as seekers is that the depth of our meditations depends to a great extent on the current health of the body. Now this won't hold true for everyone, but most of us discover that the health practices that seem to allow for a clearer and deeper meditative session include:

> Eating less red meat, shifting towards poultry and fish, and towards a higher proportion of vegetables and fruits
> Occasional fasting
> Exercising moderately, especially stretching exercises, to keep all the fluids and bio-electrical messages in the body flowing easily
> Paying particular attention to keeping the eliminations complete and regular[1]

Besides advising us to stretch "the way cats do," the Cayce discourses give one exercise of particular value for meditating. It's called the "head-and-neck exercise."

If you are doing this exercise for the first time, be careful to follow these instructions slowly. Begin by tilting the head three times forward, stretching the back of the neck as you attempt to touch your chin to your chest. Then tilt your head backward three times, lifting your head as you go so as not to come down hard on your cervical vertebrae. As you do this, feel the stretch in the front of your neck and chest. Then tilt your head three times to the left, feeling the stretch on the right side. Finally tilt three times to the right, feeling the stretch on the left side. Then roll the whole head in a complete circle, three times clockwise and three times counter-clockwise. Again, the slower the better. Feel the whole of your spine being loosened by this stretching exercise. Spinal fluid, bio-electrical nerve impulses and joints all work better after this excellent exercise.

Equally important to our practice is learning to keep our minds centered and positive. I'm sure all of us have had the experience of trying to meditate when in a bad mood or after a disagreement with someone. Sure, it can be done, but how much easier it is to get into a deep state when our outer minds are relatively peaceful and content.

One practice that can help here has been called the *fasting of thoughts,* which is just what it sounds like—the conscious selecting of thoughts that are more uplifting in nature, and the setting aside of those that are critical or negative.

Also helpful would be any time given to one's ideals, or time spent on devotional or inspirational reading. Music and incense are other ways to help you be in the best possible frame of mind for making passage (or for doing any other kind of meditation).

Not surprisingly, the arrow points both ways. Universal Consciousness is the source of life itself, and also the source of any healing we might need for the body-mind. When one person kept asking Cayce questions about certain recommended treatments, he answered:

> (Interrupting) You see, it is not that there are just so many treatments to be given and they can all be gotten through with and that's all there is to it! NO application of ANY medicinal property or any mechanical adjustment, or any other influence, is healing of itself! . . . It is the cooperation, the reaction, the response made BY the individual that is sought. Know that the soul-entity must find, in the applications, that response which attunes its abilities, its hopes, its desires, its purposes to that universal consciousness. THAT is the healing—of any nature![2]

The Body and Our Relationship with Other People

Moving now to the base of our triangle, here's a reading for Edgar Cayce himself, explaining why he should keep the body fit.

> Keep the physical fit, the soul will never die.
> Keep the physical fit that the soul may manifest the longer.
> Keep the physical fit that the physical may manifest before the physical [presence of others]. For, through the physical [manifestion of this entity], other physical beings may first gather the material benefits to themselves.

Without the manifestation of [self], none partake unless they be in perfect attune with the same forces through which this [reading] is manifested.

Keep the physical fit that the world may know that through this individual the manifestations are of the Prince of Peace.

Keep the physical fit through . . . those of the same laws as exercised by the Prince of Peace: moderation in all things, excess in none. In excess, though good or bad is conceived, the wrong impressions are given the souls of the earth plane.

Develop the soul forces by contacting those of the vibrations necessary to give the best to the Maker's realm. Present self wholly and acceptably unto all people, that none may question either the acts of the physical, the soul or spiritual purposes within this individual.[3]

What beautiful guidance: Keep the physical fit that the soul may manifest longer among those seeking help and insight into the Truth, the Way, and the Light. If we don't, then others cannot so easily gather the benefits to themselves.

In the lowest points of my life, I have felt that the only real reason for any of us to continue living (manifesting) is, as George Bailey learned in *It's a Wonderful Life*, that others' lives are made better by our continuing to be with them. This idea is especially true when we manifest the helpful, loving qualities of the Prince of Peace.

I remember one time when I was about as low as I believe we can go, I couldn't find any purpose or reason to continue. Then, in a deep period of reflection and searching, I perceived that there was one reason to go on, OTHERS! Their lives were better just by me being among them in a helpful spirit. This turned me around quickly. I understood why the readings stated that Jesus' personal prayer was, "Others, Lord, others."

I didn't have to do something big or special, just be there, in the best spirit that I could.

Today, when I get blue about aspects of my life, I remember that simple, clear purpose: keep myself fit and balanced so that I can manifest among others in the spirit of the Prince of Peace. Such a simple purpose for my existence has made such a big difference in me. When I remember this, I enjoy the moments of living among others much more.

So often, when life takes a turn for the worst, we begin to consume (to eat, to buy) in a mad search to satisfy that ache within us. But we can't satisfy it. So we eat, buy, strive for more and more, until we realize that the ache is satisfied only when we direct our life's energies beyond ourselves and toward others. Then, we find peace from our ache, and purpose for our existence. Then, the All-Giving Forces join with us in giving to others, and we are comforted and our lives are meaningful.

My body always goes off balance when I get too much into my own thing, whatever it may be; and it gets right back into balance when I take hold of that simple purpose. I begin eating better, sleeping better, living better. The little self is such an unsatisfying place to be. Self, in life with others, is a peaceful, warm place to be. I recall a reading for a young man who was practicing the spiritual methods so diligently, but he was missing something. One day, while asking the sleeping Cayce a list of big, important questions, Cayce interrupted him saying, "You think it is great to be one of the Children of God. It is far greater to be one *with* them. You are building a heaven all by yourself and you are not going to want to be there when you get there."

Keep the body fit so we can manifest among one another the longer, in the spirit of the Prince of Peace.

This does not mean that you live for others only. No. You must let your soul work on its mission in this life, too. Know yourself, your inner self, and its purpose for life now, here, with all the circumstances that surround you. Give time and energy to realizing what your inner self is driven to achieve and experience. But keep close to the simple commandments: Love God with all your being, and love others as you love yourself. Peace and happiness follow this naturally.

Applying What You've Gained from Universal Consciousness

Turning now to the right side of the triangle, we come to what is, without doubt, one of the two or three most important precepts in the Cayce readings: Live your life reflecting your inner growth. Apply what you have gained. Find an outlet, find a way to bring some of this into your outer self. Even if it simply means a different attitude that you hold, a different way you react, a different way you listen to other people, perhaps a hobby or avocation that you add to your life that somehow fits with what's occurring for you. I don't want to fix this outlet too much because there are so *many* ways we can have it manifest individually for us, and I would like you to have your own freedom to let it manifest the way it does for you. But it needs to be integrated and relevant to the outer life, integrated INTO the outer life, and relevant TO the outer life.

Since most of what Edgar Cayce said about application has to do with our relationships, let's look at a reading that I think captures the essence of his approach.

Q. I have given love and patience for three

years and my brother Jack's promises have not been kept; in fact, he has become hostile. What is the cause of this, and how shall I proceed?

(A) Hold fast to that thou hast attained. This is the fault in the other, but do not look upon it as fault; and do not be hard or severe; do not criticize but continue to give the best. Remember, as He, thy Master did, even for him who betrayed Him: He did not withhold the means of the material things given by others for the little group [Judas was in charge of the little band's money, even to the end]; neither was there a railing, neither a condemning—even with the kiss.[4]

Cayce is of course referring to Jesus' relationship with Judas Iscariot. Though the fault is with her brother, she should strive not to criticize, be hard or severe, nor withhold trust, but continue to give the best. How hard this is to do when family, friends or associates are obviously wrong. The reading goes on:

Q. Can I hope for him to help my husband as promised? Or is it futile?

A. Hold to the thought. Do not doubt. Creating doubts and fears or saying such things hinder the very activity. Just hold to that which is to the body the RIGHT![5]

Now here is a very important teaching for all of us. Cayce tells her to "hold the thought." Her own doubt and fear about her brother's help hinders the very fruition of such hopes! *Hold the thought to that which is being sought!* I have personally experienced the power of this great teaching. The reading continues:

Q. Please give me further spiritual guidance

that will enable me to meet the present trying situation.

A. Just hold fast to that ye have known, and that ye know to be good. Do not condemn, ever, others. Do not rail on others. This does not mean to be so passive as to become to the self that of self-condemnation; for this is even worse than condemning others.[6]

Again, so important a teaching is being conveyed here: worse than condemning others is condemning self. We must first be able to live with ourselves, find a certain peace within our own heart, then act from that place. Do not let ourselves be so abused that we have no self-respect. Yet, a delicate balance is being sought:

But it means doing day by day that which is KNOWN, that which is proven, that which is experienced to be in keeping with what He would have thee do. Thus ye will find that ye do the first things first; that is, the thought of self not so much as self-preservation from want, care, discouragements and the like, but rather as to just being gentle, just being kind. For righteousness, which is taking time to be righteous, is just speaking gentle even when harsh words, harsh means are resorted to by others. This is what is meant by 'Turn the other cheek,' and know the LORD standeth with thee![7]

The only way we will know the real power of what is being taught in this reading is to DO IT in our daily lives, with those around us. Then, we'll see just how amazing this approach is.

It helps to remember that on this plane, the earth

plane, God manifests only in Nature and in the human heart. We come here, in part, to make that manifestation more real, more present.

> Know that each entity enters the material sojourn not merely for the purpose of living an experience or a life, but as a part of the universal consciousness as would make the world, the earth, the individuals the entity meets from day to day, more hopeful, more patient, more long-suffering—yea, to make the world better for the entity having come in contact with the individuals the entity meets.[8]

Besides the benefits to our happiness, the application or giving out of Universal Consciousness also will deepen our meditations, by the principle that as we apply what we have, more will be given.

> Q. How could I improve my meditations?
> A. By being, as given, more and more patient, more and more long-suffering, more and more tolerant, more and more LOVELY to everyone ye meet in EVERY way ye act, in every word ye SPEAK, in every thought ye think.[9]

After a while, we begin to feel the spirit of God, of Universal Consciousness, of Life itself, *flowing through us*, from meditations to situations and relationships with often astonishing results. Love, patience, tolerance, giving are all aspects of the Spirit of God. Doing them brings us into that Spirit. That, in the end, is what our life is all about.

> In this period of man's experience in the earth there is the greater need that he, man,

consider the purposes (and the needs) of God in his daily life. There is the need for such thought, such meditation on this universal consciousness, this field, to be manifested by man's love, man's activity towards his fellow man.[10]

6

LETTERS

Spiritual Breakthrough in Action

*A*s others practiced the passage-in-consciousness technique and applied themselves to spiritual breakthrough, I began receiving letters. These letters proved to be wonderful insights into what this approach is like in action. Here are some of these letters and my comments:

From Clifford Kauffman, Greenwood, DE:
"At this point in time I have made passage in consciousness seven times (very busy schedule). Numbers five and six I experienced lapses in consciousness for decent amounts of time. Number seven was not so good. I'm very concerned about getting 'back on track.' I do

experience tremendous rushes of energy from bottom to top, and extreme sensations in pineal area. I also experience some 'free falling' in subconscious. My dreams have been getting longer and clearer. I sleep with a small tape recorder, and speak into it after dreams (three to five times a night), then the following day I enter info into a journal.

The most memorable dream was after my number six session. In the dream I met you and your secretary at the shopping center. You gave me some pamphlets. We talked about a book I had read, Jeff Green's *Pluto: A Journey of the Soul*, an amazing and informative book I wish to share with you. You and your secretary gave me a ride to another book store. In this book store I was walking through the back aisle and passed a man putting books on the shelf. As I walked by, I had a feeling about this man—I thought, 'It was God!' I started to turn around and BOOM, I woke up! No chance to fall back to sleep, but I was in a great mood all day, wondering what's going on here."

I responded:

"This is a great dream, and I have an instant sense of its meaning: 'Don't look for another book, you are walking right past Him—you are ready for direct communication and training from God.' That's it. That's the message of this dream. God puts the books out there to help seekers, but a seeker can, at any time, turn and speak directly to the Universal Consciousness of God. On that note the dream ends abruptly. Go direct, He's right there. P.S. I don't have a secretary, but I do have many helpers: Doris, Ellie, Merval, Rowena, Flo, Pam S., Peggy, Stuart, John W., Jim, Tom, Sam, Sharon and many more. Thanks to them all"—JVA

* * *

From Robin Ricci, Houston TX:

"I took your Spiritual Breakthrough course in Houston in '93. I've been practicing faithfully but I'm a bit confused. When we're raising the soul from the second chakra to the sixth chakra are we also raising energy, or am I confusing the kundalini meditation with the passage-in-consciousness practice? The reason I'm asking this is because I'm getting too much energy in my head and it's uncomfortable. Because of this I can't seem to get the transition into the Universal Consciousness that is supposed to come after the soul has arisen. Thanks for your help with this."

I responded:

"You've got it: in the kundalini meditation we raise the life force or vital energy, but in the passage-in-consciousness practice we raise the consciousness through levels. These levels are from 1) conscious level to 2) subconscious level to 3) superconscious level and then on into 4) the Universal Conscious level. We *imagine* the soul and its companion, the subconscious mind, rising from the lower portions of the body upward and expanding as it moves into the spirit and its companion, the superconscious mind. This is more an expanding dimensional movement than a bodily energy movement. Therefore, rather than energy moving into the head, we should feel our minds and beings rising into a more expansive state of awareness and beingness. The body should become suspended, rather than energized. This should actually feel pleasant and uplifting, not uncomfortable. Most of the discomfort with this practice occurs after we return and have not rebalanced the body for normal functioning in this dimension. If energy comes with this rising of consciousness, then it too should expand in an unconcentrated manner, causing no discomfort. However, unlike the kundalini meditation technique, I do not imagine or think or try to raise energy when raising my soul and subconscious in the passage-in-conscious technique—energy raising would simply be a by-product of consciousness raising."—JVA

* * *

From Michael S. Taylor, Goleta, CA:
"I am a member of an A.R.E. Study Group in Santa Barbara, and was turned onto your book "Spiritual Breakthrough" via the group. Let me say that it is a work of art! The techniques are excellent, and I have had much success with them. I have been meditating since the 70's and once in a great while I could get to the silence, now I can access it at every session! Thank you."

I responded:
"This type of sharing is so important to me and those of us practicing the methods. It validates our information, giving proof to its effectiveness. Of course, the first proof must be within each of us, but then it's good to hear that the material and methods work well for other seekers, too. Keep sharing your experiences."—JVA

* * *

From Sonja Stephens-Parker, England:
"I am finding, and this may be a combination of the Study Group work and this practice, that my dream recall is deeper and better. By this I mean that occasionally I am able to consciously bring back fragments of dreams that I had lost upon awakening. My intuition is

deepening too, as is my conscious guidance in the form of visions.

"Once, soon after starting to do the Spiritual Break-through practice, I felt the presence of Edgar Cayce close beside me. The light was exquisite and it was as though he was encouraging me."

I responded:

"I believe he was encouraging you. After all, the Spiritual Breakthrough practice is developed from Cayce's instructions for reaching the levels of consciousness that he reached in order to give a reading. Remember also that Edgar came to me while I was learning the method. We are one and there is no death, so Edgar is aware of our efforts."—JVA

* * *

From Peggy Rose Day, Mystic, CT:

"Constant practice in the 'setting self aside' aspect of your Spiritual Breakthrough technique helped im-mensely in allowing a powerful, expansive, higher energy to replace my fearful, downward-pulling personality/self.

"During one practice I had an image of a door that I didn't feel worthy to open, but then Jesus appeared, en-folded me in Himself and went through the door with me inside Him. On the other side of the door we then peeled off our skins (as the Antareans did in the movie *Cocoon*). We flew upward together, with me still inside His constantly expanding body of light—up to the Throne of a huge temple, where He went inside an even larger Body of Light. We merged with Its energy and love.

"I appreciate the references in your talks regarding the Book of Job. In having all these tough situations, I had been wondering what I'd done wrong to deserve them. Finally, I had a dream in which I asked Jesus, 'Why is all this stuff happening to me?' He smiled and answered, 'It's just to get you ready.' I woke up much relieved."

I responded:
"Wow! This is what it's all about. You and I know there was more to your dream that could not be written here, but suffice it to say that it reinforced the idea that we are going through STAGES of preparation to get ourselves ready for greater and greater awareness and service. Thanks for sharing this with us."—JVA

* * *

From Sherry Janes, Arizona:
"I received the Passage in Consciousness tape and put it to immediate use. However, I discovered right away that I needed help in mentally taking myself through the steps, especially the subjugation part. I solved this by listening to phrases you use and explanatory information, then created my own tape. I also put a brief relaxation exercise in the beginning.

"This tape helped tremendously! I was able to follow through the steps without having to think about what came next, and the sound of my own voice kept it personal.

"I did get to a point where I didn't need as much suggestion and now need a new tape.

"As to what I experienced: The very first experience was the best. I think this was because I had spent two to three hours listening to your tape and preparing my own. I was completely absorbed mentally in the process. I wasn't expecting such an energy flow, though. My journal for this experiences reads as follows:

"'Noticed feet were uncomfortable, as if full of energy,

and then hot. Moved them off of the pillow (a small sofa pillow). Seemed to help if I crossed them at the ankles. Felt energy in lower chakras. Used breathing to try to move the energy upward. This was too stimulating. Where did this energy come from? Seems as if I should expect the opposite results.

"'Had one brief moment of incredibly bright light, so bright that I winced, even with my eyes closed. Light was a small dot—gold, white and blue. This brought feelings of joy and cleansing and wanting to cry. It was too intense to maintain for more than a few seconds. Hands felt hot and full of energy. No mental impressions except one shadow of a man that briefly crossed my field of perception.'

"All of these experiences were not new to me, but with this practice, were received in a different way. I experienced that intense light many years ago during one of my very first meditations. The heat and energy in my hands are the same I feel when giving Mari-EL healings, but it seemed much stronger through the Passages practice. The feeling I had afterwards was that I had experienced healing on several levels, as well as touched something very sacred. This is turning into a belief as I continue the practice and often experience these energies. In case you're wondering, I am lying with my head to the north."

I responded:

"I too experience much energy flow. Like you, when this energy is pronounced I don't have many visual impressions. The visuals seem to happen at other moments in the practice. I believe healing and adjustments to the body are being made during these energy flow periods. Cayce does identify God with electricity, which always has a magnetic field associated with it. Perhaps these energies are realigning the "poles" within our bodies for better indwelling of the soul and spirit. This is very similar to what is predicted to happen in the outer world with the magnetic poles of the earth. Whatever the case, my body is not the same as when I started this practice. That is for sure."—JVA

* * *

From Jenny Allen, Arizona:

"I was so excited and so full of hope when I started Spiritual Breakthrough meditation. I had great success at first and then I couldn't hold my focus anymore. I found myself doing more and more thinking. I am having the same old problems with concentration and focus. But my dreams have been my state to commue with the Lord; in dreams He's always on the earth with me.

"During the practice, I attempt to hold my focus on my Crown chakra then, almost as soon as I get to my third eye center, I get images, sounds, feelings, similar to when I'm going to sleep. They are related to my life. Sometimes they're about God, but sometimes they're about my dog, school, work, just anything. If I fight they come. If I don't fight they come. If I ignore them, they come. No matter what, the thoughts come, even thoughts about thoughts!

"The most meditation-like thing I get is a wave of heat that goes up my spine, around my head and down my forehead and the front of my body. But it's not the deep healing kundalini experience that I had with my therapist, when I felt God's unconditional love within me for an hour and my eyes were healed of myopia.

Please help if you can."

I responded:

"Jenny, you are soooo close to a spiritual breakthrough! Please keep on keeping on. As the Cayce readings say, 'There's no surer way of getting there!'

Here are my suggestions:

First, I want you to realize that God is aware of you, and has and continues to manifest Itself to you, in your dreams and in your healing experience. Now here's the key to understanding your dilemma: God is manifesting Itself to your true, eternal self, your soul-self. Cayce says the mind of the soul is the subconscious—the same mind in most dreams and in your deep healing experience. It is your subconscious-soul self that knows God and God communes with. It is your outer mind, outer self, that is frustrated at not having an experience with God or a good meditation. But the scriptures tell us that this portion of ourselves does not inherit the Kingdom of God. It is the inner, soul-self that is the heir. Your outer self loves God, seeks God, but, like the crucified savior, it must die to its desires, commending its soul and spirit into God's hands. When you have completely suspended your outer self, either in sleep or in your healing experience, you have known God directly.

Long-suffering, as Cayce has presented it, includes the daily practice of laying aside the concerns and interests of this world and this earthly portion of our being. Then, as the saviour showed, the surrender leads us into the dark transition to resurrection. But the one that resurrects is not the earthly one, but the heavenly one, the soul-subconscious self.

Don't fight the loss of consciousness, teaches Cayce. It is the beginning of the awakening of soul-consciousness. Number 137 was taught that the Spiritual Breakthrough would begin with "lapses in consciousness" during the practice. Then, it would proceed to semi-consciousness. Finally, you'll become fully conscious. But the you that will be fully conscious will not be the you that surrendered. It will be the soul-you. You will have died to the old and awakened to the new. Then the real hard part begins: living it patiently each day for eternity. This results in a patient, enduring, quiet peace.

So, next time you practice, let go, die to the interests and concerns of this world. Don't try to bring God down into your outer self's consciousness. Surrender your outer self's consciousness that you may ascend into God's consciousness. In reading 311-5 an angelic being comes through the sleeping Cayce with this insight: "No one approaches the Throne or the Threshold of Universal Consciousness without the purpose of either lifting self to that consciousness or bringing us down to their own ideal." The self here is not the outer, earthly self, but the inner, soul self.

When your third eye becomes stimulated by the kundalini energy moving through you, your earthly self begins to bring up all its worldly concerns, and the images come. Before getting this far, surrender your earthly self, suspend it, remove it. Crucify desire in self that the Lord may take hold of your soul-self and awaken it. Then the Lord's agenda arises.

It takes time to do this. If I seek too quickly (less than fifteen or twenty minutes into the practice) I always end up with the outer self seeking its interests, and the meditation deals with these issues for the rest of the session. But if I am patient, surrendering, seeking to die to my interests and awaken to God's Presence (fifteen to twenty or more minutes into the practice), then when the veil drops, my soul rises—my earthly self is suspended—virtually asleep. See? It was the same for Mr. Cayce. Keep in touch. You are very close."—JVA

* * *

I received the following letter from one of our fellow seekers. She asks a question that all seekers have asked from the beginning, "What about sex? Are we to all be monks?"

"I have attempted to live a righteous path and to crucify my selfish interests. However, I am stumped as to how to deal with the sexual urge. Are we to all be monks? I have never heard where Jesus was ever with a woman in a sexual experience. Therefore, isn't that the way for all of us, since Edgar Cayce says, 'HE is the pattern'? Any advice or reference that would offer me guidance would be helpful."

I responded:
"Thank you for your letter inquiring about sex and spiritual development. You don't say how old you are or whether you're a male or female. Your name is one of those names that can go both ways—one of my best friends has the same name. It would help me to know your age and sex, but I'll answer your question anyway.

"In the Cayce readings sexual activity is an individual decision. Each person who inquired of the sleeping Cayce received an answer that related to their particular perspective on the topic. For example, a woman who had been a nun, taking a vow of chastity, for two previous lifetimes, was told that it would be difficult for her to have normal sexual activity in her current marriage because of the effect of these previous vows and their influence on her subconscious mind. However, through patience on the part of both husband and wife, they could ultimately have normal sexual relations. In a different case, a Hindu man who was living and working in the U.S. sought a Cayce reading about his prospects for marriage in this lifetime. The reading reminded the man that he didn't believe in his heart that sexual activity and marriage were the ideal lifestyle; therefore, he should not marry, remaining true to his inner belief. Another couple was given detailed guidance as to how to have good sexual relations with one another.

"Each individual has to get in touch with his/her personal feelings and beliefs about sex and spiritual development. There is no single rule that fits all people. Some can have good sexual activity and continue to develop spiritually, while others cannot combine the two.

"According to the Gospels, Jesus does state and exemplify a non-marriage position on this topic. The Cayce readings state and exemplify a pro-marriage position. St. Paul looks at it as a problem of weakness rather than choice. Yet, the Cayce readings say, "The only sin is self!" If sex is strictly for self-gratification, then it'll lead to harm and sin. But if it's in the spirit of love and togetherness, then it leads to love and togetherness.

"If you personally feel comfortable with sex and it doesn't get in the way of your spiritual development, then it is good for you. It you do have a feeling that sex is in some way incompatible with your spiritual development, then it is.

"Remember, the life force (which is also the sexual force) is in everyone, and it must be used! It has to go somewhere. Now, it can be expressed in many ways—sexual activity being one of them. Therefore, no person is without sexual urges, because no one is without the life force. But one can be expressing the life force through some other chakra, such as the heart or the mind.

"If you want to use your life force in a different manner, then you must learn how to redirect its energy. The best way to get this energy into the upper chakras is through meditation and the circulation of the life force through the kundalini path—a circular path within the body (see *The Secret of the Golden Flower* or Chapter 5 in my handbook, *Spiritual Breakthrough*). However, meditation isn't enough; you must also use the energy out here in this life in some way that gives it release or expression that is other than orgasm. It could be through creative work that requires much energy, for example. It could be through caring for others in a way that requires much energy. It could be through sport or contest that requires great amounts of energy to maintain peek levels of performance. It could be through healing that channels the energy through you and out to others. It could be through leadership or behind-the-scenes support work. There are many ways that people channel the life force within themselves. It doesn't have to be just one way, it can be a combination. This could even include sexual activity as a portion of the overall expression of the life force!

"Just remember, it's one force expressed in different ways and it must be dealt with; ignoring it only leads to trouble and illness. Each of us has to decide how we will use it. Unfortunately, most people just dissipate the energy through a life of reaction to circumstances and undirected urges—ultimately this leads to death of the body. But it doesn't have to be this way. Set an ideal that fits your heart and mind, then take hold of your life force and direct it according to that ideal. You will come alive—filled with purposeful, well-directed life, love, and creativity—with or without sexual activity.

"I hope this is of some help to you.

"With warm regards, John"

7

IN THE ARMS OF MORPHEUS

Death, Sleep, and the Sixth Sense

*D*eath is the ultimate change in consciousness.

According to ancient Egyptians, death causes the *ba* (soul) to leave the physical body and begin its journey through the underworld. In the underworld the soul's heart is weighed in the balance as the gods look on. If the heart is light, then the soul may continue its journey to the heavens. If the heart is heavy, then the soul has "unfinished business" which weighs down its ability to make the passage up to the heavens, so it wanders in the underworld seeking an opportunity to rise with the sun on a new morning. How does the soul find its way through the underworld and, if light enough, up to the heavens? The god Anubis, in the form of a jackel-headed god, guides the soul to these forgotten places. Anubis has a jackel-head because ancient Egyptians used the unique abilities of certain animals to represent metaphysical abilities. In the case of the jackel, it can pick up the scent of the way home even when we've lost it. Therefore, finding our way back through the unconscious into the land of the living-dead or up to the heavens is the "sixth-sense" that Anubis represents. Just as Jesus turned to Phillip at the last supper and told him that he knew where Jesus was going and he knew the way. Phillip cried, as most of us would, "How can I know?" The answer is that we have been there and though we have forgotten we can, using our sixth sense, pick up the scent of the trail and find our way back. Jesus' teaching that no one ascends to heaven but he or she who descended, even the Son of Man, adds to this concept that we were there and we know. The Anubis power within us can help us retrace our steps through the unconscious.

We don't need to die into order to experience the way to heaven. Sleep is a shadow of death.

The following Cayce readings shed some fascinating light on the nature of sleep. Since the sleep state, and the dreams that come from it, are so important to our Spiritual Breakthrough practice, it seems fitting that we study these readings. I have edited them for easier reading, clarity, and focus to our topic. Even so, they are particularly difficult readings, requiring our patience and concentrated attention.

> First, we would say, sleep is a shadow of that intermission in earth's experiences, that state called "death"; for the physical consciousness becomes unaware of existent conditions—save for the attributes of those that partake of the imaginative or subconscious and unconscious forces of that same body.

The sixth sense partakes of the ACCOMPA-NYING entity that is ever on guard before the throne of the Creator itself. This sixth sense is that as may be known as the other self of the entity. There is a DEFINITE connection between that we have chosen to term the sixth sense and the other self within self.

This sixth sense activity is the activating power or force of the other self. What other self? That which has been builded by the entity through its experiences as a whole in the material and cosmic world, see? It is a faculty of the soul-body itself. When the physical consciousness is at rest, the other self communes with the SOUL of the body, see?—correlating with that as the entity has accepted as its criterion or standard.

Hence, we may find that an individual may from sorrow sleep and wake with a feeling of elation. What has taken place? Through such an association in sleep there may have come that peace, that understanding, through that passage of the selves in sleep. Hence we find the more spiritual-minded individuals are the more easily pacified, at peace, harmony, in normal active state as well as sleep. Why? They have set before themselves that that IS a criterion that may be wholly relied upon. For that from which an entity or soul sprang is its CONCEPT, its awareness of, the Divine or Creative Forces within their experience. Hence they that have named the Name of the Son have put their trust in Him. He is their standard, their model, their hope, their activity. Hence we see how the activity through such sleep, or such quieting as to enter the silence, is entering the presence of that which IS the criterion of the selves of an entity!

On the other hand, oft we find one may retire with a feeling of elation, or peace, and awaken with a feeling of depression, of aloofness, of being alone, of being without hope, or of fear entering, and the body-physical awakes with that depression that manifests itself as of low spirits, as is termed, or of coldness, gooseflesh over the body [goose bumps?]. What has taken place? A comparison in that the poet has called the "arms of Morpheus," in that silence, in that relationship of the physical self to the soul. If one has set self in array against that of love as manifested by the Creator, then there MUST be a continual WARRING of those.

By comparison we find that energy of creation manifested in the Son, such that one could say "He sleeps," while to the outward eye it was death; for He WAS—and IS—and ever will be—Life and Death in one. As we find ourselves in His presence in the sleep state, we then compare—have we builded in the soul that which makes for condemnation or that which is pleasing in His presence? So, my son, my daughter, let thine lights be in Him, for these are the MANNERS through which all may come to an understanding of the activities. As was given, "I was in the Spirit on the Lord's day. I was caught up to the seventh heaven. Whether I was in the body or out of the body I cannot tell." What was taking place? The subjugation of the physical attributes in accord and attunement with its infinite force as set as its ideal brought to that soul. Then came the response, "Well done, thou good and faithful servant, enter into the joys of thy Lord. He that would be the greatest among you"—not as the Gentiles, not as the heathen, not as the scribes or Pharisses, but—"He that would be the greatest will be the SERVANT of all."

Which of these must be trained? The sixth sense? Or, must the body be trained in its other functionings to the dictates of the sixth sense?

What, then, has this to do—you ask—with the subject of sleep? Sleep—that period when the soul takes stock of that it has acted upon during one rest period to another—making or drawing comparisons that make for Life itself in its ESSENCE. As harmony, peace, joy, love, long-suffering, patience brotherly love, kindness are the fruits of the Spirit. Hate, harsh words, unkind thoughts, oppressions and the like, are the fruits of the evil forces, or Satan. The soul either abhors that it has passed through, or enters into the joy of its Lord. This is an ESSENCE of that which is intuitive in the active forces. Why should this be so in sleep and not in wakefulness? How received woman her awareness? Through the sleep of the man! Hence INTUITION is an attribute of that portion of self brought to awareness by the suppression of those forces from which it sprang, yet self is endowed with all of those abilities and forces of its Maker.

In a three-dimensional world, a material world, beings must see a materialization to become aware of its existence in that plane, yet all are aware of the essence of Life itself, as the air that is breathed carries those elements that are not aware consciously of any existence to the body, yet the body lives upon such. In sleep all things become possible, as one finds self flying through space, lifting, or being chased, or whatnot, by those very things that make for a comparison of that which has been builded by the very soul of the body itself.

Those who are nearer the spiritual realm, their visions, dreams and the like occur more often and are more often retained by the individual. For the first law is self-preservation. Thus self rarely desires to condemn self, except when the selves are warring one with another. If the ideal of the individual is lost, then the abilities to contact the spiritual forces are gradually lost or barriers are builded that prevent the individual from sensing of the nearness to a spiritual development.

Whether the body desires it or not, in sleep the consciousness physically is laid aside. As to what will be or what will it seek depends upon what has been builded. What has it associated itself with, physically, mentally, spiritually? The closer the associations in the mental and physical with the spiritual, then—as has been seen by those attempting to produce a certain character of vision or dream—these follow the universal law: Like begets like! That which is sown in honor is reaped in glory. That which is sown in corruption cannot be reaped in glory. And, the likings are associations that are the comparisons of that which has been builded. Such experiences as dreams, visions and the like are but the ACTIVITIES in the unseen world of the real self of an entity.

Ready for questions.

Q. How may one train the sixth sense?

A. That which is constantly associated in the

mental visioning, in the imaginative forces, that which is constantly associated with the senses of the body, that will it develop towards. There are NO individuals who haven't at SOME TIME been warned as respecting that that may arise in their daily or physical experience! Do they heed? Do they heed to that as may be given as advice? No! Then, it must be experienced!

Q. How may one be constantly guided by the accompanying entity on guard at the Throne?

A. It is there! It's as to whether they desire it or not! It doesn't leave but is the active force. As to its ability to SENSE the variations in the experiences, it is as given in the illustration: "As to whether in the body or out of the body, I cannot tell." Hence this sense is the ability of the entity to associate to that realm it seeks for its associations during sleep periods, see?

The subconscious and the abnormal, or the unconscious is the mind of the soul. That is, the sense that is used is of the subconscious or subliminal self that is on guard ever with the Throne itself. Has it not been said, "He has given his angels charge concerning thee, lest at any time thou dashest thy foot against a stone." Have you heeded? Then, He is near. Have you disregarded? Then, He has withdrawn to thine own self, see? That self that has been builded, that is as the comparison that must be presented—that IS presented—before the Throne itself! CONSCIOUSNESS—see— man seeks this for his OWN diversion. In sleep the soul seeks the REAL diversion, or the REAL activity of self.

Q. What governs the experiences of the astral body while in the fourth-dimensional plane during sleep?

A. That upon which it has fed. That which it has builded. That which it seeks. That which the mental mind, the subconscious mind, the subliminal mind, SEEKS! That governs.

Then, we come to an understanding of, "He that would find must seek." In the physical or material this we understand. That is a pattern of the subliminal or the spiritual self.

Q. What state or trend of development is indicated if an individual does not remember dreams?

A. The negligence of its associations, physically, mentally, and spiritually.

Q. Does one dream continually but simply fail to remember consciously?

A. Continues an association or withdraws from that which IS its right, or its ability to associate! There is no difference in the unseen world to that that is visible, except in the unseen so much greater expanse or space may be covered! Does one always desire to associate itself with others? Do individuals always seek companionship? Do they withdraw themselves? That same desire carries on in the unseen world! See? It's a NATURAL experience! It's NOT an unnatural—it is nature—it is God's activity! His associations with man. His DESIRE to make for man a way for an understanding! Is there seen or understood fully that illustration that was given of the Son of man: that while those in the ship were afraid because of the elements [the storm], the Master of the sea slept. What associations may there have been with that sleep? Was it a natural withdrawing? Yet, when spoken to, the sea and the winds obeyed His voice. Thou may do even as He, wilt thou make thineself aware of the ability of those forces within self to communicate with, understand, those elements of the spiritual life IN the conscious and unconscious, these be one!

Q. Is it possible for a conscious mind to dream while the astral or spirit body is absent?

A. There may be dreams. It's as one's ability to divide self and do two things at once.

The ability to read music and play is using different faculties of the same mind. Different portions of the same consciousness. Then, for one faculty to function while another is functioning in a different direction is not only possible but probable, dependent upon the ability of the individual to concentrate, or to centralize in their various places those functionings that are manifest of the spiritual forces in the material plane. BEAUTIFUL, isn't it?[1]

For our practical use, let's restate some of the key concepts and guidelines presented in these readings.

1. There are two selves, an outer self who usually loses consciousness during sleep and an inner self who gains consciousness during sleep. The outer self, the personality is associated with the seen world. The inner self, the soul-self, is associated with the unseen world.

2. The unseen world is no different than the seen except in the unseen so much greater expanse or space may be covered. The same desires, attitudes, and habits carryover into the unseen from the seen.

3. The inner self has a sixth sense. This sixth sense is the activating power or force of the inner self. The outer

self must be trained to subjugate its influence to the control of the inner self in order for this power to fully manifest.

4. During sleep, a review and evaluation goes on, measuring the day's activities and thoughts against a standard or criterion. If the Son of God is the criterion, then one enters into that Presence and is either pleasing or abhorrent.

5. The two selves can war with one another if the activities and thoughts of the outer self do not fit the goals and needs of the inner self, or do not measure up to the criterion held as ideal.

6. The essence of life is ever presence, even when not seen or consciously perceived, as air to a physical body. The essence of real life is harmony, peace, joy, love, long-suffering, patience, brotherly love, and kindness. Hate, harsh words, unkind thoughts, oppressions and the like, pollute the air and slowly kill the real essence of life.

7. That which is intuitive in the outer life is the essence of the inner, real life. Intuition is acquired by suppressing the outer's influence in order to allow the inner to surface, endowed with all those abilities and forces of its Maker. Thus, in sleep, when the outer is suppressed and the inner is active, all things become possible.

8. What one seeks, one finds. The inner self is ever ready to manifest, but it must be sought, desired.

9. What one feeds upon physically, mentally, and emotionally, one attracts when entering into the unseen world of sleep.

10. It is a NATURAL experience.

Now that we have some idea of the dynamics of dreaming and the development of the sixth sense, let's look at Cayce's tips for dream recall.

First, since slipping into asleep is actually a transition

from conscious mind to subconscious, and since the subconscious is so amenable to suggest, Cayce recommends that we give ourselves a pre-sleep suggestion (as we are falling asleep) to recall our dreams. Second, since the conscious mind is not having the dream and is in control of the central nervous system (which operates much of the movement of the body), Cayce recommends that we not move the body immediately upon awakening. Rather, lie still and scan your deeper mind for the dream content. Finally, once the content is present, transfer it over to the conscious mind and write it down in an ongoing dream journal. So much will be gained by this. Think of it as going to college, the college of the soul and spirit. Graduation is fully knowing yourself to be your true and complete self, and yet one with the Whole. Within you is the greatest teacher of all.

8

SHOW US GOD

*F*inally, we reach the difficult completion of our journey to God-consciousness. Humans know everything from a perspective of *separateness.* There is "I" and "you," "me" and "it." Therefore, there is "me" and there is "God." The most difficult transition to make is the movement into oneness with God. The idea that God and I are one is hard to accept. At the Last Supper, Phillip and Jesus get into this very discussion. Phillip wants Jesus to simply show him the Father, and that will be enough. But Jesus counters that it is impossible for him to separate himself from God, saying, "If you have known me, you have known the Father. The Father and I are one." This was most likely disappointing to Phillip. We know things

as either a part of our personal beingness or separate.
This is especially true of God. Few humans think of
themselves as one with God. Yet, this is the final stage in
fully realizing the spiritual breakthrough we've been
seeking.

Cayce often says, "He (Jesus) did not think it robbery
to make himself one with God." But we do. How many of
us could say, "If you see me, you see God." Yet, we are
projected aspects of God, and if we are attuned to God,
we are projecting God's spirit, will, and qualities into this
Earth realm. Try going through a day (after you have attuned yourself well to God through meditation and
prayer) as a channel of God's spirit in this realm. It's an
amazing experiment. One of the first things that you'll
notice is how quickly you affect the spirit of God with
your own concept of what God is like or how best God
should do something. It is very difficult to set oneself
aside so completely as to allow God's spirit to flow freely
through us. If you do this for some time, you'll also notice that you, the human aspect of you, does not take to
this oneness stuff comfortably. We like God to be separate. Then we can live as best we can, trusting in God,
but never fully responsible for want is happening in our
lives or other people's lives.

Imagine if you and I began to think, act, and feel as
though we and God worked together, in a oneness,
throughout the day with everyone and every situation
that came along—*equally* responsible for the outcome.
As co-creators, no situation or relationship would totally
be God's responsibility or totally our responsibility. Now
you and I are as responsible as God for everything
around us. If we believe something needs to be changed,
and we feel God's will is with us on this change, then it is
as much our job as God's. Further, if we do it *with* God's
presence consciously with us, then it is not the work of
our hands alone, but our joint work with God.

Ultimately, we must come to know that not only God is God, but we are a part of that great Oneness. God is not a separate being or power. God is in us and around us. We are in God and throughout God. God is a universal, infinite beingness and power that is composed of all beings and power. We are part of that infinite composition. God is not without us. We are not without God. Are we all of God's being? Not as long as we are in the finite, personified condition. However, we can attune ourselves to the infinite condition, and then we may know infinity, universality. The difficulty is bringing this back into this earthly realm of the finite and individual. With practice the two conditions can become one, as I believe Jesus exemplified.

We can fully realize this only through daily practice with thinking, speaking, and acting in a attuned oneness with God. This does not mean that we, our feelings and thoughts, are lost in God's. No, it is a co-creative relationship. We know ourselves to be ourselves, yet one with God—one with the Whole, the Infinite, the Universal. God knows us, and we know God, together in a oneness of purpose we live—forever.

Appendix

ABOUT EDGAR CAYCE

*E*dgar Cayce (pronounced, KAY-see) was born on a farm near Hopkinsville, Kentucky, on March 18, 1877. As a child he displayed unusual powers of perception. At the age of six he told his parents that he could see and talk with "visions," sometimes of relatives who had recently died, and even angels. He could also sleep with his head on his schoolbooks and awake with a photographic recall of their contents, even sighting the page upon which the answer appeared. However, after completing seventh grade he left school—which was not unusual for boys at that time.

When he was twenty-one, he developed a paralysis of the throat muscles which caused him to lose his voice.

When doctors were unable to find a physical cause for this condition, Edgar Cayce asked a friend to help him re-enter the same kind of hypnotic sleep that had enabled him to memorize his schoolbooks as a child. The friend gave him the necessary suggestions, and once he was in this trance state, Cayce spoke clearly and directly without any difficulty. He instructed the hypnotist to give him a suggestion to increase the bloodflow to his throat; when the suggestion was given, Cayce's throat turned blood red. Then, while still under hypnosis, Cayce recommended some specific medication and manipulative therapy which would aid in restoring his voice completely.

On subsequent occasions, Cayce would go into the hypnotic state to diagnose and prescribe healing for others, with much success. Doctors around Hopkinsville and Bowling Green, Kentucky, took advantage of Cayce's unique talent to diagnose their patients. They soon discovered that all Cayce needed was the name and address of a patient to "tune in" telepathically to that individual's mind and body. The patient didn't have to be near Cayce, he could tune-in to the patient wherever he was.

When one of the young M.D.'s working with Cayce submitted a report on his strange abilities to a clinical research society in Boston, the reactions were amazing. On October 9, 1910, *The New York Times* carried two pages of headlines and pictures. From then on, people from all over the country sought the "sleeping prophet," as he was to become known.

The routine he used for conducting a trance-diagnosis was to recline on a couch, hands folded across his solar-plexus, and breathe deeply. Eventually, his eyelids would begin fluttering and his breathing would become deep and rhythmical. This was the signal to the conductor (usually his wife, Gertrude) to make verbal contact with Cayce's subconscious by giving a suggestion. Unless this procedure was timed to synchronize with his fluttering eyelids and the change in his breathing, Cayce would proceed beyond his trance state and simply fall fast asleep. However, once the suggestion was made, Cayce would proceed to describe the patient as though he or she were sitting right next to him, his mind functioning much as an x-ray scanner, seeing into every organ of the body. When he was finished, he would say, "Ready for questions." However, in many cases his mind would have already anticipated the patient's questions, answering them during the main session. Eventually, he would say, "We are through for the present," whereupon the conductor would give the suggestion to return to normal consciousness.

If this procedure was in any way violated, Cayce was in serious personal danger. On one occasion, he remained in a trance state for three days and had actually been given up for dead by the attending doctors.

At each session, a stenographer (usually Gladys Davis Turner, his personal secretary) would record everything Cayce said. Sometimes during a trance session Cayce would even correct the stenographer's spelling. It was as though his mind was in touch with everything around him and beyond.

Each client was identified with a number to keep names private. For example, hypnotic material for Edgar Cayce is filed under the number 294. His first "reading," as they were called, would be numbered 294-1, and each subsequent reading would increase the dash number (294-2, 294-3, and so on). Some numbers refer to groups of people, such as the Study Group, 262, and some numbers refer to specific research or guidance readings, such as the 254 series containing the Work readings dealing with the overall work of the organization that grew up around him, and the 364 and 996 series containing the readings on Atlantis.

It was August 10, 1923 before anyone thought to ask the "sleeping" Cayce for insights beyond physical health—questions about life, death, and human destiny. In a small hotel room in Dayton, Ohio, Arthur Lammers asked the first set of philosophical questions that were to lead to an entirely new way of using Cayce's strange abilities. It was during this line of questioning that Cayce first began to talk about reincarnation as though it were as real and natural as the functionings of a physical body. This shocked and challenged Cayce and his family. They were deeply religious people, doing this work to help others because that's what their Christian faith taught. Reincarnation was not part of their reality. Yet, the healings and help continued to come. So, the Cayce family continued with the physical material, but cautiously reflected on the strange philosophical material. Ultimately, the Cayces began to accept the ideas, though not reincarnation per se. Edgar Cayce preferred to call it, "The Continuity of Life." He read the Bible every year, from front to back, and felt that it did contain much evidence that life, the true life in the Spirit, was continual.

Eventually, Edgar Cayce, following advice from his own readings, moved to Virginia Beach, Virginia, and set up a hospital where he continued to conduct his "Physical Readings" for the health of others. But he also continued this new line of readings called "Life Readings." From 1925 through 1944 he conducted some 2,500 of these Life Readings, describing the past lives of individuals as casually as if everyone understood reincarnation was a reality. Such subjects as deep-seated fears, mental blocks, vocational talents, innate urges and abilities, marriage difficulties, child training, etc., were examined in the light of what the readings called the "karmic patterns" resulting from previous lives spent by the individual's soul on the earth plane.

When he died on January 3, 1945, in Virginia Beach,

he left well over 14,000 documented stenographic records of the telepathic-clairvoyant readings he had given for more than 6,000 different people over a period of forty-three years.

The readings constitute one of the largest and most impressive records of psychic perception. Together with their relevant records, correspondence, and reports, they have been cross-indexed under thousands of subject headings and placed at the disposal of doctors, psychologists, students, writers, and investigators who still come to examine them. Of course, they are also available to the general public in topical books or complete volumes of the readings, even on CD ROM for DOS and Windows, and MacIntosh computers.

A foundation known as the Association for Research and Enlightenment (A.R.E.) was founded in 1932 to preserve these readings. As an open-membership research society, it continues to index and catalog the information, initiate investigation and experiments, and conduct conferences, seminars, and lectures. The A.R.E. also has the largest and finest library of parapsychological and metaphysical books in the world.[1]

The Problem Interpreting His Readings

Edgar Cayce's readings do present some difficulties in interpretation and understanding. First, they are somewhat difficult to read, mostly due to their syntax and the presence of archaic or biblical terms and style. They are *written* records of a *verbal* presentation, a process that occasionally does not carry the full intent that was expressed, and punctuation can significantly change the meaning or intent of the voiced statement. Also, most of the readings were given to specific people with uniquely personal perspectives and prejudices on the topics being discussed, and therefore, the responses were slanted to fit the seeker's perspective. For example, in a reading for one person, Cayce recommends one marriage for life, to another he recommends never getting married and to a third he encourages him to marry at least twice. In the few cases where a reading was purposefully for broader presentation to many people, even the masses, the "sleeping" Cayce was still somewhat at the mercy and wisdom of the those directing the session and asking the questions. Nevertheless, Cayce and his wife, Gertrude, and their assistant, Gladys, were very conscientious people, always seeking to be exact and true to the original intent of the reading. As I indicated earlier, the "sleeping" Cayce would occasionally stop his direct discourse to give an aside to Gladys about the way she was recording the material, correcting spelling, or giving a clarifying explanation of something he had just said. Finally, because some of Cayce's readings cover so many points or issues within the text, it can be difficult to determine which one he is referring to when the paragraphs are so complex. Despite all of this, with practice, one can become familiar enough with the syntax, terms and "thys", "thees", "thous," a repetitive use of the word "that", and the complex thought pattern, that one can learn to read and understand the Cayce readings fairly easily. Throughout this book I've edited the readings for clarity and focus to the issue we are studying.

Notes

Chapter 1

1. 5392-1
2. #262-28; also, #5377-1
3. John 8:58
4. #2156-2
5. #294-8 (#294 is Edgar himself.)
6. #5367-1
7. Luke 17:21
8. Gen. 1:26
9. #900-181
10. John 14:8-11
11. Gen. 1:2
12. Gen. 1:2
13. Gen. 1:3, EC #1947-3
14. Gen. 1:4-5
15. Psa. 19:2
16. Gen. 1:2
17. John 3:8
18. John 4:24 (The New Testament was originally written in Greek. The Greek word for spirit is "pneuma," which primarily indicates the wind or air, as does the Hebrew word of the Old Testament, "ruwach.")
19. Rev. 1:10
20. #1257-1
21. Job 33:4
22. Job 32:8-9
23. Gen. 41:38-39
24. John 14:26, 16:13
25. Deut. 6:4
26. Gen. 2:7
27. Gen. 6:3
28. Joel 2:31
29. Matt. 24:51
30. Gen. 1:26-27
31. "God" is the name in Chapter 1 of Genesis, "Lord God" begins in Chapter 2 and carries on until the name is changed to "Lord" in Chapter 4.

32. #900-227, 364-9 & -13
33. Gen. 2:5
34. John 17:5
35. John 14:2-4
36. "Chavvah"
37. Gen. 2:17
38. #2072-10
39. Gen. 2:7
40. Gen. 2:18
41. John 15:19
42. The Hebrew word for "rib" could also be translated "side," as in "a side of beef," "a rib of beef." "Side" is the more correct word for this passage.
43. Gen. 2:23
44. Gen. 2:25
45. Gen. 2:17
46. #281-33
47. #815-7
48. Gen. 3:1
49. Gen. 4
50. Gen. 4:6-7
51. Gen. 1:28
52. 2823-1
53. Gen. 3:22-24
54. John 3:3,6
55. Gen. 3:15
56. Luke 1:31-35
57. Joel 2:28
58. Acts 2:2-4
59. Ps. 36:7-9
60. John 12:27
61. John 16:21
62. Rev. 12:1-2
63. John 12:24-25
64. John 8:28
65. Moses literally means "drawn out." As the story goes, he was drawn out of the Nile river by Pharaoh's daughter (symbolizing Pharaoh's developing feminine aspect).
66. Ex. 13

67. Num. 21:8
68. John 3:13-15
69. Job 1:6
70. Job 1:8
71. Zech. 3:1-4
72. Zech. 3:9
73. Zech. 4:6
74. #1473-1
75. #281-16
76. Rev. 12:3-4
77. Rev. 20:2, " . . . the dragon, *the serpent of old*, which is the devil and Satan."
78. Rev. 12:10-12
79. #3357-2
80. Ex. 12:12-13
81. John 12:27-28
82. Mark 14:34-36
83. 1 Cor. 15:50
84. Matt. 27:46
85. Luke 23:46
86. Rev. 21:1
87. Rev. 22:1-5 and 22:17
88. #281-16

Chapter 2

1. #1861-18
2. #137-3
3. Wallace & Benson, 1973, p. 200
4. John 4:24
5. #2475-1
6. 281-13
7. John 3:14-15
8. #1299-1
9. #262-85
10. #281-29
11. #378-44
12. #2475-1
13. #2475-1
14. #281-5, -6, and -14

15. #281-29, Rev. 6:12 & 8:1
16. #281-13
17. #294-141
18. #294-140 through 142.
19. 281-24
20. 281-5
21. 281-24
22. 262-115
23. 2982-3

Chapter 3

1. #262-33
2. #262-100
3. One good example is 254-67.
4. #137-5
5. #294-140
6. #900-10
7. #137-5
8. Two examples are #294-103 & -155
9. John 4:23-24
10. Bits and pieces found in 294-103 & -140, 900-16, 1033-1, 3744-1 through -4, 5756-4, and several others.
11. #3744-1
12. #294-4
13. #3744-2
14. #900-10
15. #254-67
16. See also *Sleep and the Sixth Sense* in the Appendix.
17. Rev. 1:10-12, #281-16
18. #3744-1
19. #3744-2
20. #900-16
21. #3744-1, 2 & 4
22. #281-5
23. #262-87
24. #294-19, 254-68
25. John 16:21
26. #137-7
27. John 7:38, "Out of his heart shall flow rivers of living wa-

ter." (See also Isaiah 44:3 & 55:1.)
28.   #137-7

Chapter 4

1.   #900-16
2.   *Ibid.*
3.   Acts 9:3-7
4.   See *Sleep and the Sixth Sense* in the Appendix.
5.   #281-16 & -37
6.   *Ibid.*
7.   *Ibid.*
8.   Rev.19:9 & 10 and Rev. 22:8 & 9
9.   Psalm 82:6 and John 10:34
10.   967-3
11.   3004-1
12.   1861-4
13.   3211-2
14.   5106-1
15.   954-5
16.   2554-1
17.   1096-4
18.   262-81
19.   3744-2, edited for clarity and focus.
20.   #281-13, edited for clarity and focus.
21.   *Ibid.*
22.   *Ibid.*
23.   #137-5
24.   826-11
25.   2828-2
26.   900-181
27.   294-140
28.   *Ibid.*
29.   311-5
30.   262-15
31.   440-20
32.   2897-4
33.   900-181

Chapter 5

1. A book that covers most of these health practices is Sandra Duggan's *Edgar Cayce's Guide to Colon Care*, available through the Edgar Cayce Bookstore.
2. 2153-6
3. 294-7
4. 1000-19
5. *Ibid.*
6. *Ibid.*
7. *Ibid.*
8. 2550-1
9. 272-9
10. 262-129

Chapter 7

1. 5754-1 through 5754-3

Appendix

1. Their address and phone number are: A.R.E., 67th St. & Atlantic Ave., Virginia Beach, VA 23451, (757) 428-3588.